The DAKOTA
or SIOUX
in Minnesota
As They Were in 1834

The DAKOTA or SIOUX
in Minnesota
As They Were in 1834

SAMUEL W. POND

With an introduction by
GARY CLAYTON ANDERSON

Minnesota Historical Society Press   •   St. Paul   •   1986

Borealis Books are high-quality paperback reprints of books chosen by the Minnesota Historical Society Press for their importance as enduring historical sources and their value as enjoyable accounts of life in the Upper Midwest.

♾ The paper used in this publication meets the minimum requirements of the American National Standard for Information Sciences—Permanence for Printed Library Materials, ANSI Z39.48-1984.

MINNESOTA HISTORICAL SOCIETY PRESS, St. Paul 55102-1906
First published in 1908 in *Minnesota Historical Collections*, Volume 12
New material copyright © 1986 by the Minnesota Historical Society

International Standard Book Number 0-87351-193-X
Manufactured in the United States of America
10 9 8 7 6 5 4 3

Library of Congress Cataloging-in-Publication Data
Pond, Samuel W. (Samuel William)
    The Dakota or Sioux in Minnesota as they were in 1834.
    Reprint. Originally published: The Dakotas or Sioux in Minnesota as they were in 1834. 1908.
    "First published in 1908 in Minnesota historical collections, volume 12"—T.p. verso.
    Bibliography: p.
    Includes index.
    1. Mdewakanton Indians.   2. Dakota Indians.   I. Title
E99.M435P66 1986   973'.0497   85-31039
ISBN 0-87351-193-X

CONTENTS.

———

INTRODUCTION TO THE REPRINT EDITION.

In the fall of 1831, during the period of American revivalism called the second Great Awakening, the brothers Samuel W. and Gideon H. Pond joined a Congregational church in their home town of Washington, Connecticut, and were born again for Christ. Such conversions were not unusual at that time, and Washington had been experiencing a "great revival" throughout much of the summer. This event changed the lives of the young men — Samuel was but twenty-three and Gideon two years his junior — and they both felt the presence of a strange power. Steeped with a new unrelenting dedication, the brothers committed themselves to work for the Lord.

The Ponds found Connecticut to be a frustrating field for their labor; nearly the entire white population already belonged to churches. But both Samuel and Gideon possessed the kinds of practical skills that could be utilized anywhere — Samuel had taught school in Washington and was an excellent farmer while Gideon had learned carpentry. Thus Samuel struck out for St. Louis in 1833, unsure of his final destination but willing to place his fate in the hands of the Lord. Gideon pledged to follow when a field of labor had been discovered.[1]

On the Ohio River, Samuel contracted cholera. Rather than remaining in Missouri, a place he had at first thought promising, he

[1]Sources about the Ponds that were consulted for this introduction include: Samuel W. Pond, "Two Missionaries in the Sioux County," ed. Theodore C. Blegen, *Minnesota History* 21 (March, June, September, 1940): 15–32, 158–75, 272–83, hereafter "Two Missionaries"; Theodore C. Blegen, "The Pond Brothers," *Minnesota History* 15 (September 1934): 273–81; Samuel W. Pond, Jr., *Two Volunteer Missionaries among the Dakotas, or, The Story of the Labors of Samuel W. and Gideon H. Pond* (Boston: Congregational Sunday-School and Pub. Soc., 1893); and Edward D. Neill, "A Memorial of the Brothers Pond, the First Resident Missionaries among the Dakotas," *Macalester College Contributions*, 2d ser., no. 8 (1892): 159–98. The author wishes to thank Alan R. Woolworth for his research assistance.

traveled north to Galena, Illinois, for his health. As he recovered and began to look for work, he encountered several Winnebago Indians; later, he heard stories of the Dakota (or Sioux) people who lived farther north and west. The more he thought of the "heathen" Indians, especially the Dakota who he assumed were still relatively unaffected by the rough frontier environment that existed in Illinois, the more he came to believe that they represented the challenge that he and his brother sought. The Ponds probably shared the belief, prevalent in the East, that the Indians were diminishing in numbers and soon would disappear from North America; naturally, missionaries should save as many of them as possible before that happened. Samuel decided to go among them the next year and Gideon agreed to join him.

Samuel had come to Galena with a hundred dollars and earned more there as a gardener, but after suffering illnesses and buying supplies for the future, his money was gone. Gideon, who had worked on a farm in the summer and attended an academy in the winter, arrived in Galena on May 1, 1834, with three hundred dollars. Shortly after, the brothers departed, heading up the Mississippi River to Fort Snelling, in the heart of the Dakota country. The boat trip upriver was uneventful except for a chance meeting at Prairie du Chien, a trade center at the mouth of the Wisconsin River, where several Dakota Indians happened to be bartering with a white trader. Seeing his chance, Samuel learned from the trader how to ask in Dakota the name of an object. He then struck up a conversation with the Indians, asking them the names of the merchandise in the store. As each word was spoken, Samuel wrote it down. In such a fashion, he began his study of Dakota linguistics and culture. Working with his brother, Pond collected much of the vocabulary that lead to the publication of hymnals, many books of the Bible, and the first dictionary of the language, as well as the classic ethnographical study entitled "The Dakotas or Sioux in Minnesota As They Were in 1834," published first in volume twelve of *Minnesota Historical Society Collections* (1908) and herein reprinted by the society.[2]

While the ethnography was probably written during the winter of

[2]Publications in Dakota by various authors before 1852 include school books, hymnals, a catechism, excerpts from the Bible, and a newspaper. See J. Fletcher Williams, "Dakota Bibliography," *Minnesota Historical Society Collections* 3 (1870–80): 37–42 and Blegen, "Pond Brothers," 277–78. The dictionary was published by the Smithsonian Institution under the editorship of Stephen R. Riggs as *Grammar and Dictionary of the Dakota Language: Collected by Members of the Dakota Mission* (Washington, D.C., 1852). The spelling of Pond's title has been modernized for this edition.

SAMUEL W. POND

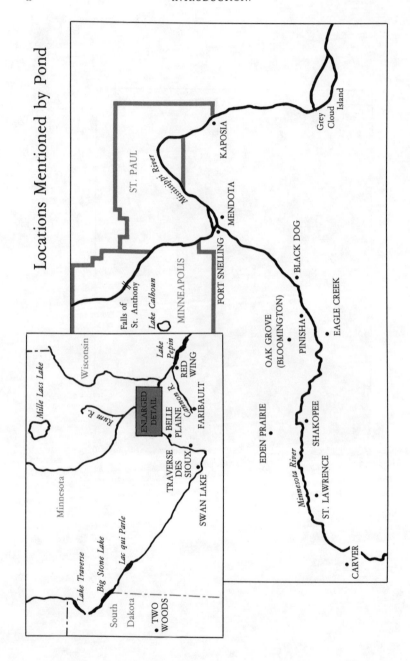

Locations Mentioned by Pond

1870–71, many years after Pond left the mission field, it is unrivaled today for its comprehensive discussion of Dakota material culture and social, political, religious, and economic institutions. Unfortunately, Pond has received less attention than he deserves, possibly because the work is often perceived as missionary literature and thus is viewed by some scholars as having an unreliable bias. Pond seemed to anticipate such criticism, stating that the main goal of the ethnography is to "show what manner of people the Dakotas were as savages, while they still retained the customs of their ancestors" (p. 3). In other words, Pond hoped — as is evident in the title he selected — to develop an objective assessment of the Dakota before their intercourse with whites dramatically changed their society.[3]

Pond's credentials for writing ethnography came from spending nearly twenty years in intimate association with the Dakota. This period of observation began in 1834, when he and his brother landed at Fort Snelling, an American military establishment at the mouth of the Minnesota River, near the present-day city of Minneapolis. The Ponds were quickly convinced by the post commander, Maj. John Bliss, to go and teach Little Crow's band of Mdewakanton Dakotas how to use a plow. The site of the band's village at Kaposia, nine miles below the fort on the Mississippi, is now part of South St. Paul.

This brief effort, which the Indians found unrewarding, brought the Pond brothers to the attention of Maj. Lawrence Taliaferro, the conscientious government agent for the Dakota. Because of the depletion of animal populations in the fur trade, Taliaferro tried desperately to convince the Dakota people to turn to agriculture. With this goal in mind, he offered the brothers a deal. He proposed that they settle near Lake Calhoun, a beautiful body of water less than a dozen miles northwest of the fort, and teach the ways of white civilization and farming to the small band of Mdewakantons living there under Cloud Man. Taliaferro purchased building materials and farm tools, using money from his own salary, and by the fall of 1834, the Ponds had a mission and a field for their labors.[4]

[3]Pond to J. Fletcher Williams, May 10, 1871, General Correspondence Files, Minnesota Historical Society Archives. The Minnesota Historical Society has a manuscript by Samuel Pond entitled "The Dakotas of Minnesota" which may be the final draft of the ethnography. The published and manuscript versions are almost identical; the manuscript also has editorial comments apparently written by Pond's fellow missionary to the Dakota, Thomas S. Williamson, who died in 1879.

[4]Lawrence Taliaferro Journal, July 7, 1834, Taliaferro Papers, Minnesota Historical Society.

The early years at Lake Calhoun were extremely important for developing the Ponds' knowledge of the Dakota people, but the slow pace of their missionary efforts proved frustrating. Language was the most difficult hurdle in bringing about mass conversions like the one that had turned the Ponds and other eastern converts to the church. Believing that such an approach would work with the Dakota, Samuel and Gideon undertook to learn their language. As 1834 came to a close, the Ponds had adapted the English alphabet for writing Dakota, using new symbols for consonants when necessary. The common Dakota consonant sounds *ch* and *sh*, for example, were simply represented by *c* and *x* respectively, and where other such changes had to be employed to distinguish pronunciation, accent marks were added. By the spring of 1835, both Ponds had made considerable progress in daily conversation. Even while not among the Indians, the brothers practiced their Dakota, learning, as Samuel once noted, to think in the language.[5] Such progress, though, was a far cry from being able to create arguments or preach Christianity, and the first full year of missionary activity passed without significant effort on the part of the Ponds to convert the Indians.

The interest in language exhibited by the Ponds soon attracted other students. Over the summer of 1835, several soldiers from the fort, a few traders, and some mixed-bloods assisted Samuel in the development of a more complete vocabulary. After a conversation with several mixed-bloods, Samuel concluded that unfortunately the knowledge of these people was often limited to a conversational language that existed primarily for commercial purposes. The mixed-blood informants failed even to understand that Dakota possessed verbs and a future tense. The Ponds, working with the Indians, soon discovered otherwise and continued to build their linguistic knowledge.[6] Studying the language so intensely also led to a better understanding of Dakota culture in general.

In the fall of 1835 Samuel was offered a marvelous opportunity to learn more of the language when the Dakotas at Lake Calhoun allowed

---

[5]Dakota became so natural to the Ponds that by the 1850s they actually felt uncertain about preaching in English. See Pond, "Two Missionaries," 281–82.

[6]Lt. Edmund A. Ogden contributed a manuscript of English words with Dakota definitions that he and other officers had compiled with the help of Scott Campbell, the fort's mixed-blood interpreter. The Rev. Daniel Gavin, a Swiss Protestant missionary at Red Wing, passed on to the Ponds what he had learned about Dakota from Pelagie La Chapelle, a mixed-blood at Prairie du Chien. See Pond, "Two Missionaries," 26–27, 159–60, 277.

him to accompany them on their October deer hunt. "The language however was the game I went to hunt," Pond later wrote, "and I was as eager in pursuit of that as the Indians were of deer."[7] The party, which included fifty Dakota men and many women and children, moved north along the Mississippi, hunting the many white-tailed deer that lived in the small river valleys of its tributaries. As Pond learned more of the language, spending much of his time in or about the lodges, he also recorded in his mind much of the detail of that hunting excursion, noting the way in which the Dakota took game and how they moved from camp to camp in search of animal herds during the fall. Pond's description of the Dakota fall hunt (p. 43–53) is unmatched for its detail and sense of understanding. Though never an admirer of the Dakota way of life, Pond did conclude after hunting with the Dakota for a month that they were an industrious and extremely skillful people.

Back at Lake Calhoun, Pond found a second problem awaiting him that at times eclipsed his struggle with the language. Two new missionaries had arrived in Dakota country, sent by the American Board of Commissioners for Foreign Missions in Boston. Thomas S. Williamson, finding that others were working near the fort, took the advice of Major Taliaferro and moved up the Minnesota River over a hundred miles to Lac qui Parle, a trading post run by a Dakota and French mixed-blood named Joseph Renville. Jedediah D. Stevens, however, the second man to arrive, settled only a mile from the Ponds at Lake Harriet. Stevens, being ordained, soon pressed the Ponds into joining him. Trouble erupted almost immediately, for Stevens was an overbearing man, convinced that lay preachers were not properly trained to correctly interpret the faith for Indians. Assuming superior status, Stevens expected Gideon Pond to build his station while Stevens studied the Dakota language.[8]

In 1836, as tensions built at Lake Harriet, Williamson asked Gideon to assist him at Lac qui Parle. Harboring suspicions of Williamson's intent, Gideon asked his older brother to travel up to Lac qui Parle and discuss the arrangement. Starting on foot in February, Samuel undertook a perilous journey through unfamiliar lands, at one

---

[7]Pond, "Two Missionaries," 28.

[8]The Ponds' difficulties with Stevens can be followed in "Two Missionaries" and in the many letters they all wrote to the American Board of Commissioners for Foreign Missions (hereafter ABCFM). Typewritten copies are in ABCFM Correspondence, Minnesota Historical Society.

point getting caught in a five-day blizzard. Much later he wrote, "It seems strange to me now that we could perform those journeys exposed to the fiercest storms and sleeping out in the coldest nights . . . but in fact we did not expect to be comfortable."[9]

Once at Lac qui Parle, he found Williamson to be much more agreeable in temperament than Stevens and even complimentary of the Ponds' success with the language. Williamson reported to the secretary of the American Board, David G. Greene, that Samuel had already developed an "uncommon proficiency" in Dakota: "He understands nearly all the words they use in their common conversations."[10] Samuel thereafter convinced his brother to join Williamson, and Gideon remained on the upper Minnesota River for three years. While Williamson also made use of Gideon's carpentry skills, the younger Pond taught school, helped translate the Bible into Dakota, and also went on a hunting excursion with the Indians. As an observer noted, "Mr. Pond had long been yearning to see inside of an Indian. He had been wanting to be an Indian, if only for half an hour, that he might know how an Indian felt, and by what motives he could be moved."[11]

On his return to the lower Minnesota, Samuel traveled south about a day's journey from the later site of Fort Ridgely to live with the Dakota then engaged in a spring muskrat hunt. He observed the Indians as they moved onto the ice-covered marshes in early morning to spear the "rats" in their aquatic houses. Each pelt was worth seven to ten cents, and the Indians were intent on accumulating large numbers in order to pay off their debts to traders. But their dedication forced them to live almost wholly on the flesh of the muskrats they killed, something that Pond found repulsive once the weather had moderated and the carcasses began rotting. Although Pond left the hunt to find food, he stayed long enough to add to his growing knowledge of the Dakota subsistence cycle.

Back at Lake Harriet, the squabbling with Stevens forced Samuel to consider upgrading his qualifications for being a missionary, if only to relieve himself of Stevens's small-mindedness. Journeying back to Connecticut, he studied with the Reverend Gordon Hayes during the summer of 1836 and was ordained as a Congregational minister the

[9]Pond, "Two Missionaries," 30.

[10]Thomas S. Williamson to David G. Greene, May 4, 1836, ABCFM Correspondence.

[11]Stephen R. Riggs, Mary and I: Forty Years with the Sioux (Chicago: W. G. Holmes, 1880), 46–47; Pond, "Two Missionaries," 31–32.

following March. He promptly returned to the upper Mississippi River and received an appointment a few months later from the American Board as a missionary to the Dakota, a position which included small amounts of financial support.

The decade that followed was one of continued linguistic work, the Ponds hoping to achieve a degree of proficiency that would enable them to preach to the Indians. They were more successful in this than the other missionaries — Stevens, in fact, would leave the mission in 1839 — and they began to tutor another student, Stephen R. Riggs, who joined the Dakota mission at Lac qui Parle in 1837. Riggs, who later published the first Dakota dictionary under his name in 1852, began his language lessons with Samuel. Riggs was taught Dakota words, as Samuel later stated with considerable satisfaction, "faster than he could learn to use them."[12] The elder Pond, however, continued to complain about his own inability to get philosophical arguments across to the Indians. "I can tell them many things concerning the character and government of God," he wrote to Greene in 1838, "but [I] cannot preach Christ crucified."[13]

Language difficulties were compounded by the many changes that occurred in the Indian community. The Lake Calhoun-Lake Harriet band of Mdewakantons fled from their village in 1839 as a result of increased hostilities between the Dakota and the Ojibway, and for much of the 1840s these Mdewakantons never established a permanent summer home. After spending most of these years following the Indians and assisting Riggs and Williamson at Lac qui Parle, Gideon settled in 1842 at Oak Grove (now Bloomington) on the north bank of the Minnesota River, about five miles from its mouth; in 1847 Samuel established a mission station at Shakopee's Mdewakanton village, some twenty-five miles farther up the river. As with previous attempts, neither of the Ponds experienced any success among the Indians, even though they attracted a few to church services on Sunday and tried to educate the children who lived nearby. Following his brother's example, Gideon went east for ordination, taking his vows as a Presbyterian minister in 1848.

Both Samuel and Gideon Pond concluded that the government's Indian policy had been partially to blame for their failures to attract converts. In 1837 the federal government had negotiated a major trea-

[12]Pond, "Two Missionaries," 160.
[13]Samuel W. Pond to David G. Greene, January 8, 1838, ABCFM Correspondence.

ty with the Mdewakanton Dakota, whereby the Indians ceded lands east of the Mississippi River in exchange for annuities. This made it even more difficult to develop farming programs among the various bands, including the ones at Lake Calhoun and Shakopee, since the government handed out food each fall. This also allowed the Mdewakantons to be less diligent hunters. Perhaps the most destructive result of the treaty, however, was brought by the whiskey dealers who moved to the east bank of the Mississippi River across from the Mdewakantons. Liquor became so readily available that it disrupted village life and made it impossible at times for the missionaries to carry on the semblance of a church or school.[14] "If we preach at all," Samuel wrote disgustedly in 1848, "we often find it necessary to preach to six, or it may be two, or even only one."[15] He took comfort only in knowing that Jesus himself delivered a sermon to a single woman standing at a well.

After the Dakota signed a treaty in 1851 by which they exchanged all their land in Minnesota for annuities, the brothers decided against following them to new reservations in the western part of the state. Samuel later wrote that he and Gideon were convinced that the new treaty would make mission work impossible. "The older Indians had gradually lost their former habits of industry or were dead," he concluded, "and a new generation had grown up of insolent reckless fellows."[16]

The Ponds remained in eastern Minnesota and undertook the responsibility of founding and serving churches for white settlers, Samuel at Shakopee until his retirement in 1866 and Gideon at Bloomington until his death on January 20, 1878. In this demanding task they were aided by their wives. Each brother married twice and was widowed once. Samuel was married to Cornelia Eggleston in 1838 and to Rebecca Smith in 1852; Gideon to Sarah Poage in 1837 and to Agnes Johnson Hopkins in 1854. All but Rebecca had worked at

---

[14]For a discussion of this treaty and its consequences see Gary Clayton Anderson, "The Removal of the Mdewakanton Dakota in 1837: A Case for Jacksonian Paternalism," *South Dakota History* 10 (Fall 1980): 310–33. Annuities are discussed in Samuel W. Pond to David G. Greene, May 10, 1842, ABCFM Correspondence.

[15]Samuel W. Pond to Selah B. Treat, December 27, 1848, ABCFM Correspondence.

[16]Pond, "Two Missionaries," 281. While this statement was influenced by the terrible Dakota War of 1862, in which five hundred whites and several hundred Indians died, it contained a grain of truth.

Dakota missions before marriage to the Ponds, and all afterwards assisted their husbands while caring for large families.

During Samuel Pond's years of retirement before his death on December 12, 1891, he turned to writing about Dakota culture and language, drawing upon his experiences with the Indians. While many whites observed and wrote about the early Dakota, Pond's ethnography is unique because he had spent so much time among these people, traveling with them and watching carefully how they lived. Pond produced two studies of his life with the Indians: this ethnography and a reminiscence of his missionary work, completed about 1880 and published in *Minnesota History* in 1940 as "Two Missionaries in the Sioux Country." While the former is certainly the more important, the latter helps us to understand Pond and gives credibility to his descriptions of the Dakota.

In the reminiscence, Pond says that he and his brother were "pioneers" in the development of the written Dakota language during a period when the people who used it were in a constant state of flux. He stresses the changes that occurred in Dakota culture directly after his arrival, explaining the cumbersome title of the ethnography. Pond also convincingly suggests that he and his brother learned more than other whites and even some mixed-bloods about the eastern Dakota — especially about their language. "Generally what was new to others," he notes, "was familiar to us."[17]

The reminiscence contains a strong criticism of Stephen Riggs, considered by many to be the foremost nineteenth-century expert on Dakota linguistics and culture. With the support of the missionaries to the Dakota, Riggs took the material for a Dakota grammar and dictionary — much of it coming from the Ponds — and published it in 1852 as his own. Although the title page states that the information was "Collected by the Members of the Dakota Mission" and identifies Riggs as the editor, his later tendency to claim authorship sparked a controversy. Clearly both the dictionary and the grammar were started and developed by the Ponds, with information contributed over a fifteen-year period by a variety of people, including Riggs. As Samuel later wrote: "There is but *one* Dakota dictionary. I have it in manuscript and Mr. Riggs had a copy of it." Understandably, Samuel found Riggs's behavior inexcusable and felt that the other missionary's reputation overshadowed and even damaged his own credibility as an

[17]Pond, "Two Missionaries," 277.

authority, especially since Pond had published so little in comparison.[18]

But Pond's accomplishments were impressive. He probably knew more about the Dakota than any other white person in the mid-nineteenth century. He spoke their language more fluently, and he was an especially keen observer of Dakota economic, social, and religious institutions. He possessed biases, which need to be pointed out, but they are less evident in his ethnography than in the observations of others. While Pond was certainly influenced by his cultural and religious background, his sense of fairness makes the ethnography a major contribution to our understanding of the Dakota.

The strength of the ethnography is found primarily in Pond's descriptions of material culture, social institutions, and subsistence patterns. His complete descriptions of clothing, tools, war implements, and dwellings have never been duplicated. For the most part, he recognizes the utilitarian value of the material items that the Dakota possessed, suggesting that these people seldom if ever carried with them or consumed more than they needed. He even praises the judicious use of jewelry by women and girls, indicating that they "wore ornaments sparingly, and exhibited good taste in selecting them" (p. 33).

Pond is at his best in the excellent description of the Dakota economy. While gathered foods provided some sustenance and Pond gives a complete list of the most important ones collected, he concludes that "by far the greater portion of their subsistence was obtained by hunting and fishing" (p. 29). While social scientists have recently emphasized gathering as an important economic function, such a clear statement regarding the consumption of protein seems difficult to refute. Indeed, the fall deer hunt, which often extended into February, provided a substantial means of support, and Pond's description of it is

[18]For Pond quotation see Pond, "Two Missionaries," 277. There are several dictionary manuscripts in the Pond Family Papers, Minnesota Historical Society. For a detailed discussion of the controversy and the manuscripts, see Williams Watts Folwell, *A History of Minnesota*, rev. ed. (St. Paul: Minnesota Historical Society, 1956) 1:447–52. Pond's appraisal of his own work appears in Samuel W. Pond to J. Fletcher Williams, September 21, 1891, General Correspondence Files, Minnesota Historical Society Archives. Apparently, both Riggs and Pond were chosen to go East and work on the dictionary, but for some unknown reason Riggs went alone. See Riggs to Selah B. Treat, September 3, 1850, and Riggs to S. L. Pomeroy, September 23, 1850, ABCFM Correspondence.

wonderfully complete. The hunt became a communal affair with every individual in the band, even children, participating.

The activity of the winter hunt seemed to represent to Pond the Dakota people at their finest. The women worked hard every waking hour to keep an orderly and mobile camp so that the men could pursue the deer. Pond is particularly defensive of the men, who hunted under extremely difficult conditions. Indeed, in several places in the ethnography, Pond strives to show that while whites often believed Dakota men to be "indolent fellows who never did anything," the men should be praised for their "industry and enterprise" (p. 65). He saw the same qualities in their efforts to take muskrats in the spring of 1836. Pond demonstrates that before the 1837 treaty, Dakota men were actively engaged in finding food for their families, having little time to linger in villages, or near Fort Snelling where they might gamble and drink.

Pond's discussions of social and religious institutions give him an opportunity to offer criticism. His analyses of family institutions — such as polygamy, the place of women in society, religious beliefs and organizations, and warfare — all provide important insights, but they frequently reveal the bias that he carried with him to the Minnesota frontier. Certainly that bias is best reflected in his assessment of Dakota religion, for Pond never doubted that Protestant Christianity was the only true religion.

Pond's discussion of Dakota religion stresses that it included many "notions" that were "confused, unsettled, and contradictory" (p. 85). It is probable that Dakota religion lacked a structure that Pond could understand and that different bands and even different Indians within bands emphasized belief systems that were most appropriate for them. Like several of his contemporaries, Pond placed too much importance upon idols and gods and gave too little attention to the positive value of spiritualism in Dakota culture.

This is best exemplified in the description by Pond of the Medicine Dance, one of the most important Dakota ceremonies (p. 93–97). He marvels at the apparent willingness of Dakotas outside the Medicine Society to accept the deception that went on during the ceremony as having real meaning. As the dance proceeded, participants frequently were "shot" with a medicine bag, fell to the ground in a seemingly lifeless state, and soon arose after coughing up a small white shell that had supposedly passed through their chests.[19] But the ceremony was ritual, supported by a belief system in which objects and acts represented a deeper spiritual truth, a fact that Pond failed to understand. (Pond did not have any difficulty in respecting the notion that during the Christian rite of Holy Communion, bread and wine represent the body and blood of Christ!)

More evidence of Pond's cultural bias surfaces in his description of feasts, a social function of major importance in Dakota society. Feasts offered an individual or a family the opportunity to demonstrate success and generosity. They also became a means of reinforcing kinship ties, the glue that held Dakota society together. In other words, a Dakota gave a feast for his or her relatives in order to show commitment and success. Sometimes food for such celebrations could barely be spared, and Pond lashes out against feasts, declaring that often food was "lavishly expended" (p. 97). But feasts were part of Dakota communal life, and members of a band saw no need to deprive themselves of such enjoyment. Food was meant to be shared, not hoarded; it was also difficult to store. Pond's criticism comes from his basic belief that nuclear family units ought to be independent and prepare for lean times. But Dakota society had no such strictures, believing that the community should survive or perish together.

One of the most interesting aspects of the ethnography is the discussion of Dakota warfare (p. 60–65, 123–37). While Pond obviously believed that the Indians were worth saving, a view held by all missionaries to the Dakota, his analysis of warfare squarely addresses one of the biggest issues confronting white Americans who thought and wrote about nineteenth-century Indians — their supposed "savagery." Writing shortly after the Dakota War of 1862, Pond felt strongly impelled to explain his views, and while this led him astray from the subject it allowed him once again to demonstrate his fairness.

Pond attempts to put Indian warfare into a broad context, comparing Dakota warriors and intertribal war to struggles that went on elsewhere in the world. "It would be easy to show that the Dakotas were not more barbarous than our ancestors," he concludes, and no less ambitious than "civilized" soldiers, who placed the same importance upon medals and symbols of honor that the Dakota did upon scalps

---

[19]Another short Pond manuscript gives a more detailed description of how new members were recruited for the Medicine Society. See Samuel W. Pond's unaddressed letter, January 22, 1841, John Howard Payne Papers, Edward A. Ayer Collection, Newberry Library, Chicago.

and eagle feathers (p. 62). Pond even defends the Dakota and their warfare: "Besides the necessity of defending their country," he wrote, "they had many relatives killed by the enemy, whose death they felt bound in honor to revenge" (p. 61). Warfare was thus no more or less warranted among the Dakota Indians than among "civilized" nations of the world. In the conclusion to his discussion of warfare, in which he gives what amounts to his general assessment of the Dakota, Pond writes: "Tried by that standard by which alone they should be tried by their fellowmen, they were a manly race, with very prominent traits of character, both good and evil" (p. 63).

As we read Pond's ethnography, we must remember the author's background and his purpose for living among the Dakota people. It is also important to keep in mind his cultural biases, especially his strong commitment to Christianity. But Pond must be given credit for his many years of dedicated study, and it should also be recalled that Pond wrote in later life, at a time when he felt a need to preserve for posterity a picture of the early Dakota people. The Dakota in 1834, especially the Mdewakantons, were much as Pond describes them, and his ethnography, read with the necessary precaution, is a unique source unmatched for its basic accuracy and understanding of the Dakota people.

GARY CLAYTON ANDERSON

The *DAKOTA*
or *SIOUX*
in Minnesota
As They Were in 1834

THE DAKOTAS OR SIOUX IN MINNESOTA AS THEY WERE IN 1834.*

BY REV. SAMUEL WILLIAM POND.

PREFACE.

Perhaps the following work needs no preface, for it is what the title indicates and nothing more. It is written because in a short time none can tell what the Dakotas of Minnesota were when the first white mission for them began. This fragment of the History of Minnesota may be of more value at some future time than it is now.

It may be thought strange that the writer, who was so many years a missionary among the Dakotas, has said nothing about the way in which they received or rejected Christianity; but he thought it better not to mention that subject at all than to treat it superficially, and justice could not be done here without too greatly extending this work. My main object has been to show what manner of people the Dakotas were as savages, while they still retained the customs of their ancestors.

---

*This paper was partly read by Samuel W. Pond, Jr., of Minneapolis, at the monthly meeting of the Executive Council, March 12, 1906. It is printed from a manuscript book written mostly during the years 1865 to 1875 by Rev. Samuel W. Pond, giving his "Recollections of the Dakotas as they were in 1834." In that year he and his brother, Rev. Gideon H. Pond, began their missionary work for these people at Lake Calhoun, building a log house there, the first dwelling of white men on the site of Minneapolis. The lives and work of these brothers were narrated by Rev. Edward D. Neill, D. D., in one of his Macalester College Contributions (Second Series, 1892, No. 8, pp. 159-198), "A Memorial of the Brothers Pond, the First Resident Missionaries among the Dakotas"; and a more extended narration by Samuel W. Pond, Jr., entitled "Two Volunteer Missionaries among the Dakotas, or the Story of the Labors of Samuel W. and Gideon H. Pond," was published in 1893 as a volume of 278 pages, with portraits and other illustrations from photographs. The author of this paper was born in New Preston, Conn., April 10, 1808; and died in Shakopee, Minn., December 12, 1891. His brother Gideon was born also in New Preston, Conn., June 30, 1810; and died in Bloomington, Minn., January 20, 1878.

SUBDIVISIONS OF THE DAKOTAS IN MINNESOTA.

Nearly all that portion of the Dakota or Sioux nation that lived in Minnesota, as the limits of the state were afterward defined, had summer residences on the Mississippi and Minnesota rivers, except those who lived at lakes Big Stone and Traverse.

There was a small village at Lake Calhoun, one on Cannon river, and one at Two Woods, south of Lac qui Parle. With these exceptions, all the Dakota villages were near the two rivers and two lakes before mentioned. This statement applies to the summer villages of the Dakotas, as during the winter months camps were made wherever deer or furs were to be found.

These Indians belonged to different divisions of the great tribe of Dakotas, and were known by different names. There were five of these divisions, namely, the Medawakantonwan, Wahpetonwan, Sissetonwan, Ihanktonwan or Yankton, and Wahpekuta.

The villages of the Medawakantonwan were on the Mississippi and Minnesota rivers, extending from Winona to Shakopee. Most of the Indians living on the Minnesota above Shakopee were Wahpetonwan. At Big Stone lake there were both Wahpetonwan and Sissetonwan; and at Lake Traverse, Ihanktonwan, Sissetonwan, and Wahpetonwan. Part of the Wahpekuta lived on Cannon river, and part at Traverse des Sioux. There were frequent intermarriages between these subdivisions of the Dakotas, and they were more or less intermingled at all their villages.

Although the language, manners, and dress of the different divisions were not precisely alike, they were essentially one people. Nor were these people of Minnesota separate from the rest of the Dakota nation, but were closely connected with those living farther west. They considered themselves as forming part of a great people, which owned a vast region of country, extending from the upper Mississippi to the Rocky mountains.

They thought, and not without reason, that there was no other Indian nation so numerous or so powerful as the Dakota nation. Before their chiefs visited Washington, many of them believed that if the Dakotas should unite their forces and act in concert, they would prove more than a match for the whites. The trip to Washington greatly modified the opinions of the chiefs on many other points, besides that of the relative strength of the white and the native races.

The reader will bear in mind that the Dakotas or Sioux of Minnesota formed but a small fraction of the nation to which they belonged, and were not distinct from the rest of their people, but are described separately because they occupied that portion of the territory of the Dakotas which is comprised within the boundaries of Minnesota and were better known to the writer than their kindred living farther west.

The Medawakantonwan were divided into eight bands. The lower band was called Kiuksa and was located below Lake Pepin where Winona now stands. The Kaposia band was at the village of Kaposia, a few miles south of the site of St. Paul. A village on the Minnesota river, two or three miles above its mouth, was called Black Dog's village; and a village named Pinisha was located on the Minnesota near the mouth of Nine Mile creek. Reyata Otonwa was at Lake Calhoun; Tewapa, at Eagle creek; and Tintatonwan at Shakopee, this last being the largest village of the Medawakantonwan.

The Wahpetonwan had villages at Carver, St. Lawrence, Belle Plaine, Traverse des Sioux, Swan Lake, and Lac qui Parle. They were also with the Sissetonwan at Big Stone lake, and with the Sissetonwan and Ihanktonwan at Lake Traverse. Most of the Sissetonwan had their villages in the vicinity of lakes Big Stone and Traverse. The home of the Ihanktonwan was at Lake Traverse, where some of them lived on islands, as the Wahpetonwan did at Big Stone lake. There was a small, restless band of Sissetonwan who lived south of Lac qui Parle.

The number of the Medawakantonwan was a little less than two thousand. The Wahpetonwan were so mixed with the Sissetonwan and Ihanktonwan that it was impossible to ascertain their exact numbers. These two divisions of the Wahpetonwan and Sissetonwan, according to a government census taken about the year 1862, numbered about four thousand; but in taking the census of the Medawakantonwan the number was greatly exaggerated, and it may have been the same with these two upper divisions.

If we estimate the Wahpetonwan and the Sissetonwan at four thousand in the year 1834, at the time to which the present work relates, we have about seven thousand as the number of the Dakotas then living within the area of Minnesota and in the part of South

Dakota closely adjoining lakes Big Stone and Traverse; for there were two thousand of the Medawakantonwan and Wahpekuta, and perhaps a thousand of the Ihanktonwan. Seven thousand may seem like a small number to occupy so large a territory, but probably not many more could have obtained a living from it by hunting.

THE CHIEFS.

Wapasha was the chief of the Kiuksa; Wakuta, of Red Wing; and Wakinyantanka of Kaposia. The chief of the Black Dog band was Wamditanka; of the Lake Calhoun band, Marpiya-wichashta; Good Road, of Pinisha; and Shapaydan (Shakpay), of Shakopee.

Mazomani was the chief of the Wahpetonwan at Carver and St. Lawrence. This little band at Carver requires a passing notice, because it led in the cowardly attack on the Ojibways at Fort Snelling in 1827. In later years they murdered a woman in cold blood near Louisville, Scott county, in 1858; and, after committing many other outrages, they inaugurated the massacre of 1862, two of them, Hdinapi and Wamdupidan, being the first to imbrue their hands in the blood of the whites. These two men, however, had married into the Shakopee band and were numbered with the Medawakantonwan.

Ishtahkba (Sleepy Eyes) was the only acknowledged chief of the Wahpetonwan between St. Lawrence and Lac qui Parle; but Wakanhdioranki was the head man at Belle Plaine, and Tankamani at Traverse des Sioux.

At Lac qui Parle, Inyangmani and Nompakinyan were chiefs. At Big Stone lake, Inkpa was chief of the Wahpetonwan, and Wakinyanduta of the Sissetonwan. Matotopa was chief at Lake Traverse. The Tizaptani had Itewakinyanna (Thunder Face) for chief. He was called by the whites Diable Boiteux, a descriptive French name, suggested by his limping gait and fiendish disposition.

When not kept together by the fear of an enemy, there was a tendency in the larger bands to separate and form smaller ones; and some of the smaller bands were composed of fugitives from the larger ones. Thus Ruyapa, having murdered a woman at Shakopee, and fearing to remain there, removed to Eagle Creek, where, gathering his relatives and others about him, he finally became a chief. The township of Eagle Creek, in Scott county, derived its name from him, the meaning of his name being Eagle-head.

The names of the chiefs who were living in 1834 have been given. Some of them died about that time, but some of them continued to hold office during many years after that date.

In a work of this kind the character of these chiefs should not be passed over in silence. As the writer was personally acquainted with most of them, he will tell briefly what sort of men they were. If the reader does not find that all of them, or any of them, are described as being very great men, let him bear in mind that we do not expect to find among any people many great men to every six or seven thousand of the population. As the office of chief was not elective but hereditary, and as the chiefs had no better education than the common people, it was not to be expected that they would be usually men of superior abilities, either natural or acquired. There were, in almost every band, others who were better qualified to act as chiefs than those who held the office, and they often had more authority and influence with the people than the chiefs themselves.

The Dakotas probably furnished their proportion of men of great natural abilities. Some individuals occasionally exhibited admirable traits of character, but in order to exhibit a savage in such a light that he will command the unqualified admiration of civilized people, it is necessary that some things in his character should be shaded or concealed and others embellished or exaggerated. Perhaps a true description of the character of the most celebrated Indians would appear more incredible to the great mass of readers than the fanciful accounts of them which have been so often published. The dealer in romance can write what he thinks his readers will believe, and can omit whatever is not likely to obtain general credence; but the relator of facts must write what he knows to be true, and, if writing about Indians, he must make statements which he knows are not in accordance with the general belief of the public. The Dakota chiefs were, some of them, noteworthy men; and, though generally inferior to some who were not chiefs, they deserve a passing notice.

Wapasha (Wabasha), chief of the band below Lake Pepin, was held in high esteem by both the whites and Indians for his good sense and upright conduct. He and many of his people died of smallpox in the summer of 1836. As the writer had no personal acquaintance with him, he can say but little about him.

Wakuta, of Red Wing, was a man not likely to be soon forgotten by those who were acquainted with him. His personal appearance was remarkably prepossessing, and his mental abilities would have commanded respect among any people. He was generally mild in his manners, but very decided in his opinions, and opposition only stirred him up to act with more firmness and determination. He was, on the whole, such a man as one would much rather have for a friend than an enemy.

Wakinyantanka (Big Thunder), of Kaposia, the father of Little Crow, was in his personal appearance the reverse of Wakuta. His features were repulsive, his manners ungainly and awkward, and his disposition unamiable. His countenance, which could never have been beautiful, had been rendered more disagreeable by a wound received in the mouth. His behavior in his youth had been so unsatisfactory that when his father died in the winter of 1833-34, Major Taliaferro, the Indian agent, did not acknowledge him as chief of the Kaposia band without great reluctance. He had a superabundance of energy and resolution, and quite enough shrewdness and cunning; but he had always an ungovernable temper, and though in some respects superior to his son Little Crow, he could never play the hypocrite so well as he.

In the spring of 1834, Major Bliss, then in command at Fort Snelling, informed me that Big Thunder had applied to him to get some plowing done at his village, but he could only furnish them a team and plow. As the Indians were incompetent to manage them, I volunteered to go down and assist in the plowing. I was to manage the oxen, and the chief was to furnish men to hold the plow. Some of the band came up and carried down the plow in a canoe, and others drove the oxen down; but when we reached the field, none were willing to take hold of the plow. They were all anxious to have plowing done, but were probably unwilling to expose their awkwardness. I had been among the Dakotas only a few days, and understood almost nothing of their language, but I could easily perceive that the chief was in trouble. I could have plowed as well, perhaps better, without their aid, but I had promised to help them only on condition that they would help themselves.

Big Thunder did not hesitate long, for as soon as he ascertained that no one else would touch the plow, he took hold of it himself and doubtless plowed the first furrow that was ever plowed by a Dakota chief. He was soon followed by Big Iron, his chief soldier, and they two held the plow alternately through the week, plowing for those who would not plow for themselves. If their strength had been skillfully applied, the work would not have been very hard for them, since they were both strong men; but they labored like men wrestling, so that it was probably the hardest week's work that they ever did.

As the work was rather hard for the oxen, it was necessary to stop them occasionally and let them stand a few minutes. During one of these intervals of rest, Big Thunder and Big Iron seemed to be in earnest consultation about something, and finally one of them took off his belt, tied it to the ring of the yoke, and attempted to lead the oxen by it, while the other held the plow. The experiment was of course a decided failure. They desisted very quickly from their undertaking when they saw how much I was amused by it. Perhaps they themselves perceived the absurdity of trying to lead cattle by the yoke while the plow was attached to it, for they both had common sense.

Big Thunder had several wives and many children. In the spring of 1841, the writer attempted to dissuade him from accompanying a war party which was then nearly ready to start from Kaposia. He was told that the course he was pursuing might bring evil on himself and his people. Many of his children happened to be present, and, pointing to them, he said, "The Great Spirit is very friendly to me; see how many children he has given me; I am not afraid of his displeasure." The next day two of his sons were killed by the Ojibways, and few of his children died natural deaths. Two committed suicide; some were killed in battle; and two were murdered at the instigation of their brother Little Crow, they having first wounded him in an attempt to take his life. Big Thunder accidentally shot himself several years before his band left Kaposia.

Little Crow inherited the restless, unquiet disposition of his father. If he had lived a generation earlier, he would probably have been an active and successful hunter, and would have passed through life without doing much harm. He was never esteemed a great man by the Dakotas, and had less influence over them than many of the other chiefs.

Wamditanka (Big Eagle), chief of the Black Dog band, was a man of not more than ordinary abilities. Nothing noteworthy in his character or career is known to the writer. He was an old man in 1834, and he may have appeared to better advantage when younger.

Marpiya-wichashta (Cloud Man), of Lake Calhoun, was not a hereditary chief. A few families settled there for the purpose of trying an experiment at farming, and as he was the fittest man among them for that office, he was appointed chief by the agent.

Cloud Man told the writer that his determination to try to obtain at least a part of his support by agriculture was first formed during a winter blizzard, when he lay buried in the snow on the prairie. He, with a party of hunters, was overtaken by a snow storm on the plains near the Missouri, and the storm was so violent that they had no alternative but to lie down and wait for it to pass over. They had a little dried buffalo meat with them, and lay separately in the snow, each wrapped in his blanket. The chief related how, as the snow drifted around and over him, he pressed it back to gain a little more room, and often made an opening through the drift over his head, hoping to find the tempest abated, but could see only the drifting snow. In the meantime he could hold no communication with his buried companions, and knew not whether they were dead or alive. During this solitary confinement he had leisure to reflect on the vicissitudes of a hunter's life, and, remembering that Major Taliaferro had the year before tried to persuade him to plant at Lake Calhoun, he determined to follow his advice if he lived to reach home again.

He was the first of the party to discover that the storm was over, and, extricating himself from his prison, he called for his comrades. He said he hardly expected to find them all alive, but they all answered to their names, though some of them were unable to crawl out of the drifts or to walk after they were taken out by their companions. They had been lying, without being aware of it, not far from a large camp of Indians, who came to their assistance.

Having reached the conclusion that it would be better for the Dakotas to turn their attention to agriculture and adopt the customs of civilized people, Marpiya-wichashta tried to persuade others to adopt his views, but with no success. It would have been well for the Dakotas if they had had more chiefs like him, but he was far in advance of his contemporaries and was the only chief who was decidedly in favor of abandoning the chase and cultivating the arts of civilized life. He was a man of superior discernment, and of great prudence and foresight. He did not hesitate to tell the Dakotas that the time had come when nothing but a change in their mode of life could save them from ruin, yet they were very slow to adopt his new notions. He was opposed by many of the other chiefs, and none of them entered heartily into his views. He was the last survivor of the chiefs of 1834 and died during the Sioux massacre and war of 1862, lamenting the infatuation of his people.

Good Road, chief of the Pinisha village, located near the mouth of Nine Mile creek, about nine miles above Fort Snelling, was an intelligent man and often appeared well in conversation; but as a chief he had not much influence, either with his own band or in a general council. He belonged to that class of persons who find it easier or more natural to complain of the manner in which things are done by others, than to propose a better way of doing them themselves. He was not so careful to avoid the use of offensive language as most of his fellow chiefs, and the undue license which he gave his tongue sometimes brought him into trouble.

In the summer of 1844 some young men of the Pinisha band or village insulted a half-breed woman, the wife of a government blacksmith, and Captain Backus, who was then in command of the garrison, ordered Good Road to bring in the offenders to Fort Snelling; but Good Road said something to the messengers which offended the captain, and he at once dispatched a company of infantry to arrest the chief.

The officer in charge of the expedition had orders to march the men to Pinisha and back in the shortest time possible. No one supposed it was necessary to send a military force to arrest Good Road. An invitation from the commander would doubtless have brought him at once to Fort Snelling, but Captain Backus said he wished to let the Dakotas know that the United States infantry could march as well as they. They were, however, more amused than alarmed by that forced march, and it is to be feared that the lesson which he was so anxious to teach the Dakotas has not been learned to this day. The march was rapid enough and the eighteen miles were passed over quickly, but several of the strongest soldiers fell out by the way and were left lying on the ground. The writer passed over the prairie with the troops on their return to the fort, and saw Good Road, who was then probably between fifty and sixty years of age, walking in advance of his captors, a little faster than his ordinary pace, but apparently with no great exertion, while his guard, both officers and men, were all panting like over-driven oxen. The offense for which he was arrested was not a very aggravated one, and he was discharged from custody soon after reaching the fort.

Shapaydan or Shakpay (Little Six), of the Tintatonwan band, whose summer village was near Shakopee, was perhaps the most widely known of the Medawakantonwan chiefs. At the same time he was the most difficult to describe so as to enable one not acquainted with him to form a correct idea of his character. Indeed, those who knew him best were often puzzled to know what to think of him. He certainly came near being a great man, and yet was a very mean one. In some respects he stood at the head of the Dakota chiefs, and in other respects he was the most despicable of them all.

He was at the same time admired and despised by all that knew him. As a speaker in council he had no equal among his contemporary chiefs. But while the advice he gave was generally good, the example set by him was often pernicious. He was of a nervous, excitable temperament, and had none of that excessive caution and dignified reserve so common among Indians, and especially among Indian chiefs.

He had moreover as little regard for appearances as any Dakota man I ever knew. He was not remarkably malicious or revengeful and was easily reconciled to those who had offended him. At times he appeared magnanimous, and some of his speeches contained sage counsel and noble sentiments; but falsehood and truth were both alike to him, and he was often detected in the commission of petty thefts, such as few Dakota men would have been guilty of,

and most of the women would have been ashamed of. It is nothing
new for a man to speak well and behave ill, to reason wisely and
act foolishly, but the eccentricities and contradictions in Shakpay's
character were certainly remarkable. By all who knew him well, he
was regarded with feelings both of admiration and contempt.

The style of his oratory will be noticed in another place. He
was not held in very high esteem as a warrior, and it was said
that he showed more audacity in council than in battle.

His son, who was executed at Fort Snelling in 1866, had hardly
sense enough to be responsible for his deeds and inherited none
but the meanest traits of his father's character. Shakpay died
before the massacre of the whites; if he had been living at that
time, he might perhaps have prevented it, for his influence with his
people was great and he always advocated the cultivation of peace
and friendship with the white people. He sometimes alarmed the
timid by the use of threatening language, but never seemed disposed
to do serious injury to any one. With all his faults, he was neither
quarrelsome nor vindictive.

While his son who succeeded him was a cipher, without character or influence, Shakpay had a brother, a rival named Hochokaduta, a bold bad man, who gathered a strong party around him during Shakpay's lifetime and had the chief control of the band after
he was dead. The first murders in August, 1862, were committed
by two or three men belonging to Hochokaduta's party. When they
reported to him what they had done, he decided to carry on the
work which they had begun and called on Little Crow for help.

Little Crow being well known, and Hochokaduta not being recognized as a chief, it was natural for the whites to look upon the
former as the leader of the murderers, and indeed he was the only
chief among them who had any influence. Still Hochokaduta was
an abler man than he, and brought much the stronger force into
the field.

The Shakpay band, not that of Kaposia, was mainly responsible
both for the inception and the execution of that bloody work. After
the massacre Hochokaduta fled north, but in the course of the
following winter he and all his family were slain by Ojibways.
Members of the Shakpay family had held the chieftainship through
many generations, and their band was the strongest among the
Medawakantonwans.

Concerning Mazomani of Carver the writer knows nothing worth recording.

Ishtahkba (Sleepy Eye), as has been already stated, was the only man recognized as chief between St. Lawrence and Lac qui Parle. There were several small villages along the river without chiefs, fragments separated from larger bands. Sleepy Eye lived in summer near Swan lake, but was often at Traverse des Sioux. He appeared to be a thoughtful, prudent man, of placid temper and good understanding. He was called a good chief and was respected by his white acquaintance, but the people who were accounted his were so scattered that he could exercise little authority over them, and the inhabitants of each little village were left to manage their own affairs in their own way.

Itewakinyanna (Thunder Face), chief of the Five Lodges or Two Woods band, was a noted character in his day, a bad leader of a bad band. If his character was not better than his reputation, it was bad enough; but though his people could not well have chosen a worse chief, probably they would not have tolerated a better one. They were as restless and roving, and supposed to be as lawless, as prairie wolves. They were good buffalo hunters, but bad horse thieves, and a terror alike to friends and foes. Though Thunder Face was at their head, it may be that they would have gone farther and done worse without him; for Indian chiefs sometimes seemed to be leading their people when they were only guiding them, as a man when he can no longer hold a runaway horse, still tries to steer him the safest way.

Inyangmani of Lac qui Parle was a better man than chief. He was intelligent and could appear well in conversation, but could not or would not speak in public to the people when they were excited and turbulent, so that his influence was felt least when it was needed most. He was chief in name but not in fact, for while he was silent, others ruled the multitude.

The writer had so little acquaintance with the chiefs at lakes Big Stone and Traverse that he will not attempt to describe them.

There were other men among the Dakotas who were perhaps more worthy of notice than the chiefs who have been mentioned, but my aim is to give a general description of the Dakotas as a people, rather than to write biographic sketches of individuals.

WHITE MEN AND HALF-BREEDS.

A description of the Indians would seem incomplete if it made no mention of the white men and half-bloods residing among them.

Henry H. Sibley took charge of the trading post at Mendota in 1834, and had the general superintendence of the affairs of the American Fur Company among the Dakotas of Minnesota. Besides trading with the Indians near Mendota, he furnished traders at remoter stations with merchandise and received from them their furs.

At Mendota the furs were counted, sorted. repacked, and shipped below. The establishment there was the point of rendezvous for all the employees of the Company, and the Indians were in the habit of resorting to it from all parts of the country. Mr. Sibley kept an open house, extending a cordial welcome to all comers, and there were few, either white men or Indians, for a long distance around, who did not at least occasionally pay him a visit.

His hospitalities were extended to others besides residents in this country, for every one from below, drawn hither by business or curiosity, found for a time a home at Mendota; and if he wished to go farther into the interior, he was furnished with such supplies, escort, and commendations, as secured his comfort and safety on his journeys. This generous hospitality was continued until the change in the condition of the country rendered it impracticable and unnecessary.

The exercise of hospitality was not confined to the headquarters of the Fur Company. At each trading post, the traveler was made welcome and received all needed aid to speed him on his way. These old traders were as attentive to the wants of their guests as is the worthy landlord who is animated with the hope of gain.

The frontier post of the Company was at Lake Traverse, where Hazen Mooers was then stationed. He had spent many years at a station still more remote on the Sheyenne river, but that post had been abandoned as too remote. Those who were well acquainted with Mr. Mooers could hardly help regretting that it should have been his lot to spend so much of his life among savages. When, after the war of 1812, the Northwest Fur Company was forbidden to employ foreigners within the territory of the United States, except as common laborers, Americans were advertised for, and Mr.

Mooers, who was a native of the state of New York and was at that time acting deputy collector of customs on the Canadian frontier, went to Montreal and engaged himself to that company for three years. On his return home he found that the collector, by whom he was employed as deputy, was about to resign and intended to recommend him as his successor. He now regretted his engagement and applied to have it canceled, but, failing in that, he came west determined to stay but three years. He was sent far west to the Sheyenne, and when his time expired he was persuaded to stay a while longer; and finally, like most who engaged in the fur trade, he never went back but died among the Dakotas in 1858, aged about seventy years.

He attempted to leave the Indians soon after they ceded their land on the east side of the Mississippi, and opened a farm on Grey Cloud Island, which derived its name from Mrs. Mooers, who was a half-breed. He was industrious but not parsimonious, and had too many Indian visitors, who shared with him the products of his farm, so that he did not succeed as a farmer, and he returned to the Dakotas as an employee of the Government.

No ordinary man could have discharged all the duties which were imposed upon Mr. Mooers by the Company while he was young. When first engaged in trade, he transported his goods in boats from Prairie du Chien to the upper Minnesota, and thence overland to the Sheyenne river. The returns, including many heavy packs of buffalo robes, were of course brought back over the same route. In a high stage of water, and when the current was strong, there were many places where the boats could be forced up the river only by catching the bushes on the shore, by means of iron hooks attached to long poles. Nor was the descent of the stream always without difficulty. He once had his boat sunk and all his furs thrown into the river at Patterson's rapids.

This long journey back and forth had to be made every summer, and a great portion of the winter was spent in traveling from one Indian encampment to another, gathering furs. In the meantime the Canadian voyageurs were to be held in subordination without law or judge, and such an ascendancy must be maintained over the wildest savages of the western plains as would render it safe and profitable to trade with them.

The writer, when on a foot journey in the winter of 1835-6, received some sage advice from Mr. Mooers which perhaps saved his life. Two items of the counsel then given him are here recorded for the benefit of others: first, if attacked by what is commonly called snow blindness, lie down on the back immediately and put snow on the eyes until the pain ceases; second, when overtaken by a violent snow storm on the open prairie, encamp at once, and do not attempt to travel until the air is so clear that you can keep the right course.

Mr. Mooers was a man of good judgment and retentive memory, and was a close observer of men and things. He could have furnished valuable materials which would have served to fill up many a blank space in the history of Minnesota, but such materials are not much valued until, like ancient coins, they become very rare. He was succeeded at Lake Traverse by Joseph R. Brown, a man too well known to the public to need mention here.

The next trading post this side of Lake Traverse was at Lac qui Parle, where Joseph Renville was stationed, who had, during many years more influence with the Indians of the upper Minnesota river than any other man. His mother was a Dakota woman. It has been said that in his boyhood he was taken to Canada and committed to the care of a Catholic priest for instruction; but if this was true, his tutor sadly neglected his duty, for he did not even teach his pupil to read. Excepting his ability to speak French, he had no education which could give him the influence that he acquired.

Renville's ascendancy over the Dakotas was chiefly due to aspiring ambition, joined with native qualities of character which enabled him to carry out his plans successfully. Employed in his youth by Lieutenant Pike and others as interpreter and guide, he had given good satisfaction and had received high commendations. The marked attention which he received from both American and British officers, he would naturally and perhaps justly regard as proof of his superior abilities.

When the writer first saw Mr. Renville, he was about fifty-five or sixty years of age, and had lost the vigor and vivacity of youth. He was short in stature, and in features and complexion he strongly resembled the full-blood Dakotas. Though there were many better looking men among the Dakotas, he was very dignified in his bearing, knew when to be reserved and when to be sociable, and seemed never to forget that he was a great man. To the very few whom he regarded as his superiors he was very deferential; and toward those whom he looked upon as inferiors he was generally patronizing, though sometimes imperious.

Perhaps no man ever spoke the Dakota better than he, and in rendering the French into that language he had no equal. He had a select body of young men, formed into a sort of society. which he often feasted and harangued in a very large tent prepared for that purpose. Their adherence to him and devotion to his interests added greatly for a time to his importance; but their mercenary services, though they gratified his vanity, cost him more than they were worth.

I once had an opportunity to witness some of the services performed for him by these men, while I was riding in a wagon with him and his family from Lac qui Parle to Traverse des Sioux. I drove the horses, and when they mired in a swamp, Mr. Renville told me to sit still and let them alone. It seemed a strange time to sit still while the horses were floundering in the deep mire and water, but I obeyed. Soon the Indians who were traveling with us came, released the horses, and drew us out to the dry ground. This was repeated as often as was necessary on the journey. Mr. Renville affected to regard these extraordinary services with indifference and as a matter of course, but he was evidently very much gratified by them.

But while we were riding so comfortably through the swamps, I was surprised to see that one of Mr. Renville's daughters, an unmarried girl, who drove one horse and a cart, was permitted to do her own wading. She was, however, a hardy, independent damsel, and had probably chosen the mode of traveling which pleased her best.

In the spring of 1839, Joseph R. Brown had a serious difficulty with the Indians at Lake Traverse, and they wounded him, killed his teams, and placed him so that he could not bring away his furs. He applied for help to Mr. Renville, who sent his son with his Indians and teams to bring away Mr. Brown and his furs. As there were apprehensions of resistance on the part of the Lake Traverse Indians, the writer asked Mr. Renville if it would not be better for him to go himself. He replied, "I have sent my name by my son and that is enough," and it was enough.

He was for a time in possession of a large amount of property, and his establishment at Lac qui Parle was quite extensive. He owned a hundred head of cattle, twenty or thirty horses, and a flock of sheep. The sheep and cattle were being driven through from Missouri to the British settlement on the Red river when their owners were driven away by the Indians, and he gathered up the stock, but he informed me that he afterward paid for them.

The family of Mr. Renville was large, and his dependents were numerous. Travelers received at his house a cordial reception and friendly entertainment, and he gave much to the poor, many of whom he had always with him. He lived to see his property all dissipated and himself neglected by many who had profited by his generosity and flattered his vanity during the days of his prosperity. Renville was certainly a man of superior natural abilities, and he had many admirers; but the most prominent traits of his character were such as belonged rather to a Dakota than to a white man.

The next permanent trading post below Lac qui Parle was at Traverse des Sioux, and was occupied for thirty or forty years by Louis Provencalle. He was commonly called Le Blanc by the whites and Skadan by the Indians, both names signifying the white man. Though a native of Canada, he was a genuine Gaul, and had all the external politeness and internal fire of a native Frenchman, as much as though he had been born on the banks of the Seine. He was vivacious, jovial and bland, but it was said that he was not remarkable for the placidity or equanimity of his temper. It was said that once when greatly enraged at the loss of his chickens, he had skinned an unlucky wolf alive. This last statement must appear incredible to those who saw the old gentleman only in his best moods. He received the casual visitor, though a stranger, with a courteous welcome, and on his departure, accompanying him to the door, or farther, dismissed him with a friendly Adieu.

Provencalle spoke the Dakota language with fluency and force, but with bold violations of grammatical rules. He was aware that his manner of speaking was not faultless, and he once told the writer that, to please his sons, who thought they could speak much better than he, he had tried them a little as interpreters, but found that though their speech might sound better to the Indians than his, it made less impression on them. He had come to the conclusion that, notwithstanding his grammatical blunders and bad pronunciation, no one could speak as well for him as he could speak for himself, and said that he should do his own talking while he was able.

In the winter of 1835-6, while I was detained at his house for a day or two by a cold wind and drifting snow, he brought forward his account book and requested me to write in it the names of his debtors. Some of the names were already written, probably by his son, who was then absent. The book was certainly a curious specimen of ingenuity. Le Blanc (Provencalle) told me that he met with no serious difficulty in keeping his accounts, except in writing the names of his customers so that in case of his death others should know who were meant. So far as the charges were concerned, one could, with the key to the book, soon learn to read it, for each kind of goods had a specific mark or figure. When practicable he drew a rude figure of the article, and when the thing could not be thus designated, some arbitrary mark was substituted, and a particular meaning assigned to it. This mode of keeping accounts had one advantage over others, in that the Indians could easily learn to read this picture writing and see for themselves how their accounts stood; but the old gentleman told me he had met with an insurmountable difficulty in attempting to write the names of persons so that others could read them. His pictures answered very well for recording most names derived from visible objects; for instance, for Chanrpiuha, he could make the picture of a man holding a warclub, which expressed the meaning of the name. But he could not write such names as Whistling Wind, Thunder Face, etc., so that any but himself could read them. He told me that he considered his attempts to write such names a failure, and so did I, but I did not think the failure due to any lack of genius. I wrote the names, but the hieroglyphics were retained for his use, as he could not read my writing better than others could his.

Le Blanc was very industrious and economical, and had accumulated some property; but he found it easier to acquire property while his children were young than to keep it after they were grown up, and this was the case with many of the fur traders.

The children of the traders were the aristocracy of the land, and naturally considered it beneath them to engage in the pursuits of the Indians, or in the employment of common laborers, while there was nothing else for them to do by which they could earn a livelihood. At the same time their position seemed to render it fit that they should live in better style than the Indians and voyageurs; and, spending much while earning little, they soon ran through the property acquired by their fathers, and were left without either means of support or ability to take care of themselves. Some of them, who had an opportunity to engage in business, instead of spending what others had earned, accumulated property for themselves; but as a class they were placed in circumstances very unfavorable to the cultivation of frugal and industrious habits.

In 1834 Philander Prescott commenced trading at Traverse des Sioux in competition with Le Blanc. He was a native of New York state, like Mr. Mooers, and came to this territory as clerk of the sutler's store at Fort Snelling when he was about eighteen years of age. He was an industrious man, but made frequent changes from one employment to another. He was at one time engaged in the service of the American Fur Company, was afterward an independent trader, and after the treaty of 1837 he opened a farm at the mouth of the St. Croix, on the Wisconsin side, where the town of Prescott now stands. He was not successful as a farmer, and brought less property away from Prescott than he carried there, but left his name as a perpetual memorial.

After Mr. Prescott's return from the St. Croix, he was employed as Government interpreter at the Agency several years and lived in the vicinity of Fort Snelling. He finally accompanied the Indians to the Reserve, and was there killed by them in the massacre of 1862. Though at the time very unwell, he fled from the Lower Agency on foot and alone toward Fort Ridgely, and had nearly reached the fort, when he was met by some Indians of his acquaintance. They appeared friendly, and after conversing with him a minute, passed on as if they did not intend to molest him, but turned and shot him in the back. Prescott lacked some of the personal qualities which a white man living among the Indians at that time needed to enable him to restrain them when turbulent and unreasonable, but he was a man of mild and pleasant disposition and had many friends. Even his murderers seem to have been ashamed to have him know that they intended to kill him, for they did not attack him in front, although he was unarmed, feeble, and defence-less.

Jean Baptiste Faribault traded at Carver, and his son Alexander on Cannon river, but they both resided most of the time at Mendota. After the father died, the son resided in the town of Faribault, which was founded by him, and where he died in 1882. As he will never see this, I will record here that Alexander Faribault was a favorite with all who knew hi..a.

At the lower end of Lake Pepin lived Louis Rock (or Roche), a French Canadian, who traded with the Kiuksa band. In the spring of 1837 the writer was his guest for a week, and though he never saw him afterward he always retained a pleasant remembrance of his frank, courteous manners and generous hospitality. A short time before, Jack Frazer and others had killed a Sac Indian, and, as was common in such cases, the Dakotas were in constant alarm, expecting the Sacs to return the visit. One evening there was a report that the enemy was near, which caused great excitement among the few Dakotas who were there at that time. Mr. Rock did not seem to be much terrified but was quite animated, as he called out to his sons, "Chargez les fusils, arrangez les haches," etc. The alarm was a false one, and the guns and hatchets were not needed.

I have been thus particular in speaking of the old traders, be-cause they were important characters here thirty or forty years ago. They, with their dependents, were almost the only representatives of the civilized world in this far-off country. The old trading posts were not regarded with indifference by the traveler, for, from one end of the land to the other, he found no other shelter from the in-clemency of the weather, except the little, crowded tepees of the Indians, and they had no fixed abiding place more than the wild buffalo.

If a traveler sought food and shelter in an Indian camp, he might find only the tepee poles, or, if on the prairie, not even these, where the Dakota tents had stood the day before. But the trading establishments, which have been mentioned, were always there and always open to all who needed food and shelter.

Mention has been made only of those posts which were permanently occupied on the Mississippi and Minnesota rivers by the American Fur Company, but there were posts of other traders, not connected with that company, called independent traders.

Mr. D. B. Baker established himself near the noted spring by the Mississippi about a mile above Fort Snelling, and did a large business furnishing goods to many independent traders. He supplied traders both among the Dakotas and the Ojibways. He built the first stone house erected in Minnesota, except those belonging to the Government.

After Baker's death, which occurred in 1839, he was succeeded in business by Hon. Norman W. Kittson, since mayor of St. Paul, who for many years did an extensive business in the fur trade.

At the time of which I am writing, in 1834, Major Lawrence Taliaferro was Government Agent to the Dakotas. He was appointed to that office in 1819, and resigned in 1840. He was a man of generous, friendly disposition, and was more popular with both whites and Indians than agents usually are. He was very gentle in his treatment of the Indians, being averse to the use of harsh means in dealing with them. Perhaps the prompt severity of the commanders of the garrison sometimes needed to be tempered a little by the mildness of the agent. Some thought that he was too lenient, but the persons and property of the whites were certainly as safe during his term of office as ever after. He once stated, in a paper which was published, that during the twenty-one years of his residence here no white person was killed by these Dakotas.

Taliaferro did not always give satisfaction to all, but he was probably more popular with all classes of persons than any who have since held the office of Indian Agent in Minnesota. He was so affable in manners and social in disposition, and continued here so long, that there were few persons living in what is now Minnesota, who were not acquainted with him. The poorer class of whites received many little favors from him and were sorry to part with him, while the Indians long deplored the departure of Mazabaksa, as they called him. He died in Pennsylvania, his native state, in 1871.

While we remember Taliaferro, we cannot forget his interpreter, Scott Campbell, a half-breed, who was a boy when Lewis and Clark passed through the country of the Dakotas on their exploring expedition. Lewis, taking a fancy to the lad, took him with him on his return to the states. After the murder or suicide of his patron, Campbell returned to his own people; and when the writer first knew him, he was Government Interpreter at the Agency near Fort Snelling. He is gone, but his old acquaintances will not soon forget him; and he had many acquaintances, for he was not only interpreter for government officials, but was also the general medium of communication between the Indians and all officers and privates at the fort who wished to converse with them. Young officers, having abundance of leisure, often had dealings of one kind and another with the Indians, using Scott Campbell as their interpreter, and he was ready to say almost anything in Dakota, French, or English, whenever it would accommodate others or add a little to his own scanty salary.

In the winter of 1834-5, Lieutenant (afterward Major) Ogden, and other young officers, by the aid of Campbell, obtained quite an extensive list of Dakota words with their meanings in English. They went through the English dictionary, taking all the words which Campbell thought he could render into Dakota. The writers labored under the disadvantage of having no suitable alphabet, and many of the definitions were inaccurate; but the work was very valuable to us who were then learning the Dakota language, and we thought the young lieutenants had spent their leisure hours to good advantage.

Ogden gave his carefully written manuscript to my brother, Gideon H. Pond, and myself, and we could not have found any other book or manuscript in any language that would have been so acceptable as that was. With considerable labor, we learned from the Indians the correct pronunciation and signification of the words; and when they were written in our new alphabet, which we had just completed, these words and definitions, with what we had gathered from other sources, made quite an encouraging beginning of the Dakota and English Lexicon which was long afterward edited by Rev. Stephen R. Riggs and published by the Smithsonian Institution.

Mr. Campbell was, in his general deportment, very mild, quiet and gentlemanly, always ready to smoke or chat with white men or Indians, carefully avoiding all harsh language and disagreeable topics; but he had a fiery temper which sometimes broke through the smooth external covering in such ebullitions of passion as we might expect from one in whom were mingled the Scotch and Dakota blood.

He was skillful as an interpreter, and perhaps more skillful as a mis-interpreter. When translating for Major Taliaferro, he gave a true rendering of what was said, for the major knew the Dakota language too well himself to be deceived by an interpreter; but for those who were ignorant of the language he sometimes used his own discretion in the choice of what to say. The words of the speaker, whether Dakota or English, lost all their asperity, and often much of their meaning, in passing through his interpretation. He told what he thought the speaker should have said rather than what he did say, and frequently a good understanding seemed to have been restored, simply because there had been no understanding at all. The grievous words which stir up strife might go into his ears but did not come out of his mouth, especially when it was for his interest to restore peace between the contending parties. This readiness to substitute his own language for that which he professed to translate might not be the best qualification for an interpreter, and sometimes it proved mischievous; but he doubtless intercepted many harsh and passionate words, which, if they had reached their destination, would have done more harm than good.

Scott Campbell no longer sits smoking his long pipe, and conversing in low tones with the listless loungers around the old Agency House; but who that resided in this country thirty or forty years ago can pass by the old stone houses near Fort Snelling and not think of Major Taliaferro and of his interpreter?

The white men and half-breeds have been thus briefly noticed, since they, with many others who must be passed over in silence, formed a few years ago a very important part of the population of Minnesota. Many of them were men of no ordinary ability. The American Fur Company did not entrust thousands of dollars' worth of goods to irresolute, rash, or weak-minded men, to be carried hundreds of miles away from all protection of law and authority, where all might be lost by the action or inaction of a stupid, rash, or timid man.

Those who had been long employed at the outposts of the Company were familiar with wild adventures and desperate emergencies, so that they came at last to regard them as ordinary events, hardly worth relating; and one might be with some of them for weeks without learning that they had ever met with any but the most ordinary occurrences. If they were more irregular in their habits and erratic in their conduct than were those whom they had left behind them under the restraints of civilized society, this irregularity should be attributed to their peculiar situation.

Their occupation is gone, and as a class they have passed away; but it is not long since they, with their jolly, reckless voyageurs, were the only white men who passed up and down these rivers, and back and forth across the prairies of Minnesota. The steamboat has driven away the boatman's barge, and the railroad train has superceded the fur traders' carts.

Doubtless these changes are all for the better, but there are a few of us yet left, who cannot banish recollections of the past, if we would; and we sometimes almost wish that, instead of the shrill scream of the steam whistle, we could hear again the merry song of the boatman, and see, just once more, our old friends the traders, each one at his post.

Food, Agriculture, Game and Fish.

Before the sale of their lands east of the Mississippi in 1837, the Dakotas of Minnesota lived almost exclusively on the products of the chase and fishing, with such vegetable food as grew spontaneously. At most of the villages a very little corn was raised by some of the families, but only enough to supply them with food for a few days. Before 1834, no land had been plowed by or for them, except a little at Lake Calhoun. Mr. Renville's relatives raised a little corn at Lac qui Parle, but only a little. More corn was raised at that time at Lake Traverse than anywhere else among the Dakotas. Mr. Mooers, who had been there many years, had persuaded the Indians to plant corn. Major Long found him at Lake Traverse, and mentions the corn fields which he saw.

In 1835 the Indians at Lake Traverse seem to have raised a surplus of corn, for Joseph R. Brown bought large quantities of it, some of which he carried seventy miles to Lac qui Parle and sold for a dollar a bushel. But in 1834, except at Lake Traverse, there was very little corn or anything else raised here by the Dakotas.

All the ground planted by them was dug up by the women with hoes. They usually selected a place where there was a thrifty growth of wild artichokes, as they were likely to find the soil in such places rich and mellow. They began by digging up a little conical mound for one hill, and then another by it, and so on, without any regular rows, till the little patch was dug over.

They never planted until they found ripe strawberries, and then soaked their seed corn till it sprouted, planting it with their hands quite deep. As soon as it showed three or four leaves, they loosened the earth around it with their fingers, and when it was large enough hilled it up thoroughly with hoes. They usually planted a small kind of corn that ripened early, but they had larger kinds and often raised good crops.

To the ripening corn the birds were more troublesome then than now, but scaffolds were erected in each field for watch-towers, and, as the fields were small and close together, the women with the help of their children, kept off the blackbirds, of which two species were abundant, one wholly black, the other red-winged. A peculiar cry, heard only on such occasions, announced the arrival of a flock of birds, and, being joined in by all the watchers, was continued until the birds withdrew.

So little corn was then raised by the Dakotas that some of the bands ate all they had while it was green, and many did not plant at all. Some of their corn was preserved by boiling it before it was hard, scraping it from the cob with mussel-shells, and drying it. What was not devoured before it was ripe, they husked, leaving two or three leaves of the husk attached to the ear, and, braiding it in strings four or five feet long, hung it in the sunshine to dry. When it was thoroughly dry, they spread their tents on the ground, and putting the corn on them, shelled it by pounding with clubs.

The corn that was not to be used immediately was put in barrels made of bark, and buried in the ground to be dug up when needed. It was usually left buried until the owners returned from the deer-hunt in January, and was so concealed that, when the snow was on the ground, none but the owners could easily find it.

The Dakotas planted little else but corn, and probably did not raise enough annually on the Mississippi and Minnesota rivers to feed the whole population more than a week or two. But they obtained considerable quantities of vegetable food which they found growing wild. Of course they gathered berries, plums, nuts, etc., wherever they found them; and they also made use of many plants as food which are neglected by the whites.

Of these native food plants the most important were the psincha, the psinchincha, the mdo, the wild turnip or pomme de terre, the water-lily, and wild rice. The psinchincha is a root, in shape resembling a hen's egg, and about half as large. The psincha is spherical and about an inch in diameter. They both grow at the bottom of shallow lakes, and the former sometimes grows in marshy ground, where there is not much water. These roots and those of the water-lily were dug, some by the men but more by the women. They often gathered them where the water was waist-deep, feeling for them with their feet at the bottom of the lakes.

When a psinchincha is detached from the mud, it immediately rises to the surface of the water; but the psincha does not float, and must be raised by the foot until it can be reached by the hand, a difficult operation, requiring much dexterity where the water is up to the arms as it often is where they grow. Formerly scores of women might be seen together in shallow lakes, gathering these treasures of the deep. As they could not dig these subaqueous roots with their skirts on, they wore instead an indispensible article of male attire. The work was disagreeable, but their families must be fed.

There is a root growing on dry land, which they called mdo, the name which they gave potatoes. It is the root of a slender vine which coils around weeds growing near it, and resembles the sweet potato more than the common potato. It frequently grows as large as a good sized potato, and, when of the right age, is very good; but it is nowhere very plentiful, and can seldom be obtained in any quantity without great labor and perseverance.

About the headwaters of the Minnesota river, the wild turnip grows singly, scattered over the prairies, and was an important article of food. These roots were dug, one by one, from the hard ground with a sharp stick, costing much labor. Indeed it was slow and hard work to collect any of the roots that have been mentioned, and frequently a peck of them cost a hard day's work.

In some parts of the country the Dakotas harvested considerable quantities of wild rice, which is both palatable and nutritious. It was collected by two persons in a canoe, one propelling the canoe while the other bent over the heads of rice and beat the seeds into the canoe with a stick. The rice was separated from the chaff by scorching it in a kettle and then beating it in a mortar made by digging a circular hole in the ground and lining it with deer-skin. If the work was done by men, they trampled on the rice with their feet; if by women, they beat it with the end of a stick.

When food was scarce, the Dakotas ate acorns and the vine of the bitter-sweet. They also obtained an article of food by boiling hickory chips, and thus extracting the sap. There were other vegetable productions eaten by them, which have not been mentioned; but by far the greater portion of their subsistence was obtained by hunting and fishing.

Mr. Oliver Faribault told the writer that he purchased in one year fifteen hundred deer-skins from the bands of Shakopee and Carver. As the Indians used many of their deer-skins for domestic purposes, these two bands must have killed during that year more than two thousand deer. This seems a large number, but the meat would not last them long, for there would be but two or three deer in the whole year for each individual, and a man will soon devour a deer when he has nothing else to eat with it. Some of the best hunters killed sixty or more deer in a year, but such success in hunting was rare.

Next in importance to deer as food were ducks and geese, and in some parts of the country they were perhaps of even greater importance.

Occasionally a few elk were killed. Two of these animals were killed while crossing the Minnesota river at Bloomington, about the year 1840. They were, however, seldom seen near that river.

Bears were occasionally found in considerable numbers, but the hunt for them was uncertain, since they wandered about the country in search of food, having no particular place of resort, so that the Indians never knew where to look for them. In the winter, several bears were sometimes found in dens not far from each other, lying partially torpid, with their heads near the mouths of their dens, and were easily killed; but successful bear-hunts were not of very frequent occurrence.

The Dakotas in the western part of Minnesota hunted buffalo, and many of them frequently came eastward to the Big Woods in winter in quest of deer.

Besides the animals mentioned above, they of course ate many smaller ones, but there were some which they did not eat except in case of necessity. They ordinarily ate few birds or quadrupeds which are considered unfit for food by white men.

It is well known that dog-flesh was considered a delicacy by them, but it was seldom eaten except on great occasions. The writer had determined never to taste canine flesh, but his Indian friends contrived to have him eat it unwittingly, and he was compelled to admit that it was very good. The exploring party of Lewis and Clark, when they were at the mouth of the Columbia, learned to prefer the flesh of Indian dogs to that of any other animal, but they did not find their own dogs so good to eat.

Horses were eaten by the Dakotas when threatened with starvation, and some of them ate such as were killed accidentally or by mischievous persons.

Muskrats were esteemed good food in winter and early spring, but not in warm weather.

Fish and turtles were consumed by them in great quantities, but they did not like to be confined to a diet of fish. In fishing they used hooks and spears in summer and winter. In the spring many fish were killed in the lakes and rivers, and in the small streams where they went in immense numbers to deposit their spawn. The suckers which they took at such times they preserved by drying them over fires.

In the winter they cut holes through the ice, and, crouching down with their blankets spread over them to exclude the light, waited patiently for the fish to approach the aperture where they could spear them. Sometimes they used bows and arrows instead of spears, a string being attached to the arrow so that it might be drawn back again. Winter fishing was most practiced by the upper Indians, they sometimes depending a long time on fish alone for subsistence. It was tedious, dreary work on the large lakes in cold weather. When the writer once said to a man, who had been fishing on Lac qui Parle one very cold day, "You were a brave man to go on the lake on such a day," he replied, "I don't know whether I was brave or foolhardy."

Frequently when the snow closed up the cracks in the ice, the fish, to avoid suffocation, crowded together at springs, and were easily taken in great quantities. When the fish could find no opening in the ice, they either made one by crowding in immense numbers to one point, or many of them smothered and in the spring were thrown upon the shore by the waves, when they were gathered up and eaten by the Indians if found before they were spoiled.

The Dakotas had a large tract of country from which to draw their supplies, and, before they received annuities, were more energetic and industrious than is generally supposed, but they often suffered for want of food. Unsuccessful hunting parties, from Lac qui Parle and other places in that region, sometimes lost numbers by starvation. In the winter of 1834-5 the Indians at Carver were in a state of great destitution, and provisions were sent to them from Fort Snelling. Such cases of destitution were not rare, and the traders relieved the most pressing wants of the natives when it was in their power; but, at the frontier posts, the traders themselves often suffered from want of provisions. The occasional scarcity of food was not always to be ascribed to the indolence or wasteful habits of the Indians, but is incident to the life of a hunter, whenever game is scarce and the cold severe. They sometimes suffered the most when they were making the greatest efforts to support themselves; and their longest journeys in pursuit of food, if unsuccessful, were the most disastrous.

DRESS AND ORNAMENTS.

So many have seen the Indian dress that a description of it may seem superfluous, but it will soon be seen no more, and the native dress as now worn is not exactly in the fashion of 1834.

The entire dress of the Dakota female consisted of a coat, skirt, leggings, moccasins, and blanket. The coat of a woman was made of about two yards of printed cotton cloth. The sleeves were tight, and it was fitted closely to the body, but was sewed up only an inch or two on the breast, the neck being bare and the coat open at the lower end. The skirt was made of a single piece of blue broadcloth, the ends being lapped and sewed together, but not across the whole breadth. It was supported at the waist by a girdle, the cloth being doubled under the sash, the outer fold not hanging so low as the inner one. By changing the length of the outer fold, this skirt might be shortened or lengthened to suit the taste or necessity of the wearer. The skirt was worn smooth in front and behind, but was gathered at the sides. The lower end reached about half way from the knee to the ankle, but was often lower than that; and when the wearer was walking in deep snow, or through grass and bushes, it was worn shorter.

The reader will perceive that what is said about Indian women having no weight of garments to carry on their hips is without foundation in fact, for in this respect they had no advantage over white women.

Their leggings were made of red or blue broadcloth, reaching from the knee to the ankle, fastened at the upper end with garters, and tucked into the moccasins at the lower.

There was no covering for the heads of females except the blanket. Some had their coats for winter made of woolen cloth, and others wore more than one cotton one; but both women and girls might be seen chopping wood in the coldest weather without mittens, and with nothing on their arms and shoulders but one thickness of cotton cloth. The blanket, however, was either fastened to their waists or lying near by, ready to be wrapped around them as soon as they had chopped what wood they could carry.

The dress of the Ihanktonwan women differed somewhat from that which has been described. Their skirts reached to their arms and were supported by shoulder straps, leaving their arms bare. Among the upper Indians many females wore leather garments instead of cloth.

Dakota women of this part of the country wore the most convenient dress that could be devised; and, except that the coat needed a few more stitches in front, it was decent and becoming. The common dress has been described, but let not the reader imagine that because they were all Indian women, their wardrobes were all alike. Some were much more costly than others. An Indian woman of my acquaintance was offered fifty dollars for her blanket, which offer she refused; and her husband told me that it cost more than that. Many other Dakota women had blankets nearly or quite as costly. They also often had other costly garments. The blanket referred to was made of fine blue cloth, heavily and tastefully adorned with silk ribbons of various colors. Some had a band of embroidered work, a foot or more wide, running around the bottom of their skirts, consisting of silk ribbons of diverse colors, folded together and laid on in such a manner as to present a variety of figures, with a blending of different colors, among which the more glaring colors, such as red or yellow, by no means predominated. The colors and figures as they were selected, combined, and arranged by them, were not such as we should have expected from persons of coarse, uncultivated tastes.

Besides the embroidery work of ribbons and beads with which they profusely decorated many of their garments, they wore other ornaments, some of which were of silver or imitation of silver, among which were thin, circular plates, two or three inches in diameter, worn on the bosom, often many at once, so that the breast was nearly covered with them. The necks of many of the young women were loaded with beads, and their ears with earrings. My brother once ascertained, by weighing, that one girl wore seven pounds of beads on her neck at once, which, however, was extravagant even for an Indian girl.

Many of the Dakota women and girls wore ornaments sparingly, and exhibited good taste in selecting them. When many beads were worn, they were so arranged, by making the strings of different lengths, that they covered the throat and breast.

Their hair was combed smoothly back and braided in two braids, one behind each ear, the ends of the braids hanging down on the breast in front.

The females used little paint. The young women put a little vermilion on the top of the head where the hair was parted, and, with the end of the finger, painted a small red spot on each cheek. The women, when young, were few of them very beautiful or very ugly, and many of them made a fine appearance when in full dress.

The Indian women, however, all had plenty of work to do, and could only occasionally find time to exhibit themselves or display their decorations. Their ornaments and costly raiment were not worn every day, but were carefully treasured up to be worn in some great assembly, as at a medicine dance or some other great meeting, where they would not shine in vain; for there are some slight points of resemblance between the red squaws whom we despise and the white ladies whom we admire.

It is not to be understood, from what has been said, that the Dakota women were ordinarily arrayed in goodly apparel, for it is the gala dress of the aristocracy that has been described. Always many of them were destitute, not only of ornaments, but of comfortable clothing. All wore plain garments when about their ordinary business, and middle-aged women made little use of ornaments; but the girls would have them if they could get them, for "Can a maid forget her ornaments?" even though she be an Indian maid.

The clothing of the men was doubtless well suited to their mode of life, but we can hardly regret that the time is near when such clothing will be no longer needed. They wore heavy blankets of coarse wool, and of dimensions suited to the size of the wearer; for these blankets were made expressly for them, and of all needed sizes. They were generally white, but some were red, green, or blue. They preferred the white for hunting, believing that the game was less afraid of them.

In cold weather the Dakota men frequently wore buffalo skins when traveling; and, for some of the old and feeble, blankets were made of deer-skin dressed with the hair on, because they were warmer than cloth and lighter than buffalo robes.

In summer the men wore shirts made of cotton, and in winter they wore, over these shirts, coats made of blankets, reaching to the knees. The coats were without buttons, and, being lapped in front, were fastened by one or more coils of steel wire, such as they used in drawing charges from their guns. These garments were warm and serviceable, but must have been very plain, for a woman could make one in three or four hours.

Their leggings were nearly as long as their legs, and were supported by straps fastened to their girdles. The lower end was made to fit the top of the foot, and, being drawn down tight over the moccasin, was fastened by straps which passed under the hollow of the foot. They were made of buckskin in winter, but in wet weather cloth was preferred; and in cold weather both cloth and leather ones might be worn at the same time.

The breech-cloth was made of blue woolen cloth, about a foot wide and three or four feet long. It passed between the legs and under the belt in front and rear, the ends hanging down a foot or more, like an apron, before and behind.

In winter they wore hoods made of white blankets, though some of the young men preferred blue broadcloth.

Their mittens were very large, of the skin of some animal tanned with the hair on, and were fastened together with a cord passing over the shoulders. When they wished to use their hands, as in shooting, loading their guns, cutting up game, etc., they drew them out of their mittens, which were used only to keep the hands warm while walking. The women used cloth mittens when cutting dead grass out of the snow for their tents, but most of their work they did bare-handed.

The socks, both of men and women, were simply oblong pieces of blanket wrapped skillfully around the foot. When expecting to walk far, they put fine, dry grass in the moccasin under the foot, which by its elasticity protected the foot and was a help in walking.

They girded up their loins by wrapping their blankets around their waists and binding them fast with girdles. The lower end of the blanket, double in front, reached about to the knees, and the upper part was wrapped about the head and shoulders, protecting all the upper part of the body and also the hands and face. There could be no better defense against the cold, for the body, hands, and face, than an Indian blanket or buffalo robe, worn in the Indian fashion; nor a better protection in extreme cold weather, for the feet and legs, than the Indian leggings and moccasins.

Hunters wore very different moccasins from those found in the markets. The dress moccasins of the men were garnished with porcupine quills, beads, and ribbons; and many other articles of male attire were elaborately decorated by the women. The bonnets for men, the apron part of the breech-cloth, their leggings, knife sheaths, and shot-bags, were ornamented with quills, ribbons, or beads; but these showy decorations were prized only by the young, and were discarded by the middle-aged and old.

Men cut off their hair across the forehead a little above the eyes, but wore the rest long. Not a few had curly hair, but neither males nor females patronized curls. The young men braided their hair in two braids behind, and also had several small braids hanging down on each side of the face, to which were fastened many small metal ornaments.

They spent much time in painting their faces with various kinds of paints, and carried little mirrors hanging to their girdles, of which they made great use. The females were told that if they looked in mirrors their eyes would be spoiled, but there were other reflectors besides looking-glasses, and probably most of them knew how they looked. None but the young men spent much time at the toilet, and not all of them were fops. The older men did not braid their hair often, but confined it with a band tied around the head. They were most of the time bareheaded, and their hair, when not braided, was a great defence against the cold.

Young men often wore skunk skins, unseemly ornaments, tied to their ankles.

When hunting or traveling, each man carried with him a bag made of the skin of a mink, skunk, or some other small animal, tanned with the hair on. These skins were taken off entire, with the head, feet and tail attached to them, the carcass being taken out through a hole cut in the skin of the throat, and the aperture thus made served for the mouth of the bag. It was suspended from the waist by thrusting the head under the girdle, and was of great importance to the owner, for it was the only pocket an Indian had. In it were carried the pipe and tobacco, the touchwood, flint, and fire-steel. All these were important articles, for without them there could be no smoking, and what was worse, especially in winter, no fire. This was called the "fire-steel bag," and they carefully guarded against losing it or having the contents wet. They were as careful of it, when away from home in cold weather, as an elephant is of his trunk.

The clothing of the men was well enough, comfortable, and convenient; but the hunter often returned wet from the melting snow or from wading streams, or from hunting around lakes or marshes, so that his garments, at least his leggings, must be pulled off and hung up to dry. This stripping off their clothes from necessity soon became a habit. An Indian, especially an old one, when the weather was warm and he was at home, never liked to wear anything that he could do without, and he could do without everything except the breech-cloth, which alone was indispensable. Much of the time he wore nothing else, but let us give him credit for keeping on his one garment. If he had been as shameless as savages are in some parts of the earth, he would have stripped that off too, which he never did. When most naked he was better clothed than even the females of some savage tribes.

Dwellings and Furniture.

The Dakota houses for summer residence were made of bark, supported by a frame of poles. In building them, they first set small posts in the ground, inclosing as large a space as the house was to occupy. These posts were set a foot or two apart, and were about three inches in diameter. On the sides of the house, they were five or six feet long reaching to the eaves, and on the gable ends they were longer toward the center, reaching to the roof. Strong forked posts were set at each end of the house, and, if necessary, one in the center, to support the ridgepole. The upper ends of the rafters rested on the ridgepole, and the lower ends on horizontal poles, which were fastened to the tops of the posts at the sides of the house. Small poles were placed transversely across the upright posts and the rafters, and were tied to the latter with basswood bark, so that the whole frame was a kind of wickerwork made of poles crossing each other at right angles. The covering of the house was taken from standing elm trees, a single bark being taken from each tree. The pieces of bark were five or six feet long and of different widths, according to the size of the trees from which they were taken. The bark was thick and some of the pieces were very heavy when green, being five or six feet square. They were fastened to the transverse poles with basswood bark, and the whole house was covered with them. Those on the roof were lapped like shingles. The poles were all peeled, and the houses, when new, looked very neat. The doors were in the ends of the house, the larger houses having a door in each end, and the small ones having but one.

On each side of the interior of the house, running the whole length of it, and on three sides if there was but one door, a bench was constructed, about two feet high, covered with bark, and in some places spread over with buffalo robes and mats. These bench-es or bedsteads were five or six feet wide, and on them the inmates of the house sat, ate, and slept.

Much of the labor of building was performed by women, but they were aided by the men who always put on the roof, that not being considered proper work for women. The roofs were waterproof, and the houses were quite comfortable in summer, the only season in which they were occupied. They were made of different sizes, according to the number and ability of the builders. Some of them were occupied by two or more families, some by a single one. The fire was built on the ground in the center of the house, and the smoke escaped through an aperture left in the roof.

A Dakota tent or tepee of ordinary size was made of eight dressed buffalo skins, sewed together with sinews, and when set up was of a conical shape, about twelve feet in height, and ten or twelve feet in diameter at the bottom. When a tent was to be set up, three poles a little longer than the tent were tied together near the top, and were set up standing some distance apart at the bottom. Nine other poles were next set around in a circle, leaning at the top against the three first set up. The tent, or tepee covering, was then laid on the ground at full length, so folded that when it was raised by means of a pole attached to the top, it could be quickly spread around the standing poles and fastened together with pins running through loops. In the center of the tent, a space for the fire three or four feet square was fenced with sticks of wood, outside of which the ground was covered with hay, and that was spread over with buffalo robes except on the side toward the door.

The side of the tent opposite the door was considered the place of honor. The owner of the tent and his wife usually occupied one side. The woman sat nearest the door, for the purpose of being near the cooking utensils, and for convenience in reaching the wood which lay just outside the door. Lady visitors did not pass by the men, but sat down between them and the door, though no space in the tent was interdicted to women; and when men were not in the way, they sat where they pleased. I have many times seen those who were engaged in needlework occupying the place opposite the door, while men were in the house. The tent belonged not to the man but to the woman, and she occupied that part of it that was the most convenient for the work she had to do. None were permitted to stand upright in the tent when it could be avoided. The tents were nearly white when new, and were translucent, but old ones were dingy and dark.

When whole, well set, and warmed by a good fire, the tent or tepee was tolerably comfortable even in the coldest weather; but new ones were costly, and the poorer families often lived in old tepees that were cold and uncomfortable. On the whole, no better dwelling for summer or winter could be devised for hunters, than those used by the Dakotas. They used no candles, but selected the dryest wood for their fires and split it very fine, so that it might give light. For a momentary light they used bark torches or a wisp of hay lighted.

On their hunting excursions, the Dakotas could carry but little furniture and it was useless for them to own much more than they could carry, for, if left behind, it was in danger of being stolen. Kettles, dishes, and spoons were indispensable; so were buffalo robes and pillows, and these were about all the articles of household furniture that they always kept with them. If they had buffalo robes and pillows to sleep on, one kettle for boiling food and another for bringing water, and a dish and spoon for each member of the family, they could get along very well, though some families always carried with them some other little articles of furniture. They used no beds except mats, skins, and blankets, but each one had a pillow of feathers. When a party of men went out to hunt a few days without their families, they carried little or no furniture with them.

They used wooden dishes and wooden or horn spoons, both of their own manufacture, and their kettles were of sheet iron. The spoons were used as dippers to drink from. They did not use forks, but each one carried a knife in a sheath under the belt.

Tools and Weapons; Manufactures.

They used no agricultural implements except hoes, which were narrow but heavy and strong and furnished with short strong handles for digging in the hard ground. The hoes were used more for other purposes than for planting, and were carried on their journeys, to be used in leveling the ground for their tents, digging roots, and so forth.

Their axes were light, being narrow at the head and widening toward the cutting edge. They were made to receive a large, round handle, for such a handle as we use would have been too weak to answer their purpose. In splitting a log, they struck the ax under a thin piece of wood and pried it off.

Both hoes and axes were made of various sizes, some for strong women and some for little girls. Armed with these axes or hatchets, women would cut down trees averaging two feet in diameter or even more, to get a few dry branches. They were very particular about their wood, and, before venturing to take any of which they stood in doubt, were in the habit of cutting out little chips and putting them in their mouths, to ascertain whether they were sufficiently dry.

They had awls for sewing leather and needles for cloth. For sewing cloth they used thread, and sinews taken from the backs of deer were used for sewing leather.

Men made little use of any tools except such as were needed in hunting and war. For edge tools they had little beside hatchets and knives, and with these they made whatever they manufactured of wood. The knife, which was ground only on one side, served for draw-knife and plane, and in whittling they drew it toward them. cutting, when they wished to, very straight. The hatchet which they carried with them when hunting was very small, was tucked under the girdle, and was used in cutting animals out of hollow trees, killing wounded deer, etc. Tomahawk and scalping-knife were nothing more than the common hatchet and knife.

Young men occasionally carried bows and arrows, but more for show than use, except as they sometimes did mischief with them, such as shooting horses. Arrows, however, were much used by some who hunted buffalo. The boys all had their bows and arrows.

The men used smooth bore guns much more than rifles, and it was a considerable time after the percussion lock was introduced, before they learned to prefer it to flint. They manufactured shot from bar lead by melting and pouring it through a sieve of perforated bark held over water, the sieve being jarred while the lead was running, so that it fell into the water in drops.

They made great use of steel-traps, but some animals they caught in wooden ones extemporized for the occasion. In fishing they used spears and hooks, but no nets.

No weapons were used only in war except spears and war-clubs. The spear had a traditionary importance, and was probably one of the weapons most used by their ancestors. In modern times, however, Dakotas did most of their fighting with guns, knives, and hatchets.

The war-club was a flat piece of wood, two and a half feet long and nearly or quite an inch thick. It was made of hard, heavy wood, often hickory. At one end it was small enough to make a convenient handle, and at the other end about four inches wide, the broad end bending back much like the breech end of a gun stock. On the outside of the bend, six or eight inches from the end, an iron like a spearhead was inserted. The broad, heavy end was designed to give force to the blow. These clubs were highly ornamented, and were carried a good deal about home, as canes are carried by gentlemen who do not need them, but the war-club was not depended on much in battle.

The head of their spears was of iron, eight or ten inches long and an inch and a half wide in the broadest part, fitted to a slender wooden handle about five feet long.

A few generations earlier, we should have found among the Dakotas a great variety of articles of their own manufacture; but after the introduction of iron among them few things were manufactured by them, except such as were made of wood or leather.

Among the articles which they still continued to manufacture, may be enumerated canoes, dishes, spoons, saddles, cradles, snowshoes, pipes, and many other small articles. Everything they made themselves was well made. There can be no better canoes than those made by the Dakotas, from the trunks of trees, with no tools but an ax and a little clumsy adze. Their wooden dishes were well formed and valuable. They were made of hard knots cut from the sides of trees, hewn into shape with a hatchet, and finished with a knife bent at the end. Their spoons and ladles were made in the same way, but provided with a handle. Their snowshoes were admirable specimens of skill and ingenuity, and their saddles were strong and durable, having well-shaped frames, covered with leather.

Their cradles or boards for infants were simple things, and a carpenter with suitable tools and materials could soon have made one. The Dakota had to get his board out of a tree with a hatchet and finish it with a knife, yet it was as well made as though from a cabinet-maker's shop. Without any suitable tools they made arrowheads from iron hoops; yet these arrowheads, hammered out with stones, could not be improved in appearance and value.

Barrels were made by bending broad pieces of bark around like hoops and lapping the ends together, sewing them with bark. The bottom was made of a circular piece of bark sewed on, and when the barrel was filled the top was covered in the same manner. These bark barrels held from two to five bushels, and in them they deposited their corn when they buried it. They were neatly made, light and strong, and when kept dry were durable.

Indeed, there was no awkwardness or bungling about anything they were in the habit of making, but all was neatly and skillfully done. The tools used by them seemed altogether inadequate to the work. It is true that they were not all alike skillful, but those who could not do mechanical work well would not do it at all and employed others to do it for them.

Pottery lately found in the territory of the Dakotas has been pronounced the work of some other people, because it was so well done, but that is the very reason why it should be ascribed to them. I have seen specimens of it, and certainly it is no better than was to have been expected at their hands. They who have seen the ornamental work of Dakota women will admit that much of it is tastefully designed and skillfully executed. They would admire it if they knew the disadvantages which the artists had to labor under, working in their dark tents, with hands that were most of the time employed in the rudest labor, which laid down the ax and hoe to take up the needle.

The most remarkable specimen of ingenuity found among the Dakotas is the cloth which was woven by the women from yarn of their own manufacture. They not only wove the sashes and broad garters worn by the men, but also cloth more than half a yard wide, made of yarn of various colors, so woven that it presented a variety of regularly shaped figures. Such cloth their ancestors, they say, made of yarn spun from the bark of nettles, or from basswood bark which had been softened by boiling; but after they obtained woolen cloth, they made yarn from that when the cloth was worn out. This invention was the more remarkable because there seems to have been no pressing necessity for it. They did not wear this cloth, but made of it bags resembling carpetbags, which were highly prized and in which they kept their best raiment and their ornaments. A few years ago almost every woman had one or more of them, of which they were very careful. They are not yet entirely superseded, as they probably will be soon by trunks and bandboxes. The proverb says, "It is the first step that costs," and certainly the Dakotas had taken the first step and a very long one, toward the manufacture of cloth.

DOMESTIC ANIMALS.

Their domestic animals consisted of a few horses and many dogs. Some families owned three or four horses, but more had none, and those who owned them often lost them. They did not feed their horses, except that they cut down trees for them when the snow was deep, and many starved to death when out in the winter on hunting expeditions. Some were killed by hard usage, others by the envious or spiteful, and so many died or were killed that always many families were destitute of them.

Dogs were abundant, and many of them were a great help to their masters in hunting. They were used somewhat as beasts of burden by the Indians on the upper Minnesota river, but were not so used by the Medawakantonwan.

THE DEER-HUNT.

It is a prevalent opinion that Indians in a savage state spend most of their time in idleness, and those who have known the Dakotas only since they have received annuities for their land may suppose that they never made much exertion to obtain a livelihood; but if they had accompanied them through one year, in 1834, they would have learned that they did not contrive to live without hard labor, also that they did not shrink from hard work, but acted like men who were determined to take care of themselves and their families. If they had been as indolent and inefficient as many think they were, we should never have heard of them, for they would all have perished long ago.

In tropical countries, where houses and clothing are not needed and food in abundance grows spontaneously, man may live without much labor, but not in Minnesota. Neither the farmer nor the hunter can get a living in this climate without working for it. The Indians have lived here for generations, supported by their own exertions, and they have also lived in colder latitudes than this. Around the frozen shores of Hudson bay and far up toward the Arctic ocean, without cloth or iron, they lived and multiplied, as also over all the plains of Minnesota, Dakota, and the Nebraska country, and far away to the Rocky mountains. Even now some branches of the Dakota people, with hardly any arms but those of their own manufacture, are a terror to the whites. Whatever may be alleged against them, they are not to be charged with imbecility.

To show how they were in the habit of spending their time, I will give a brief description of their occupations, beginning with the deer-hunt. This hunt commenced in October, for though they killed a few deer at other seasons of the year, their principal deer-hunt was in the fall and winter.

Having procured, as far as they were able, the needed supplies of clothing, guns, ammunition, etc., the various bands started in different directions, the larger subdividing into smaller parties, that they might spread over a larger extent of country, for they needed all the game to be found within their territories. They held the land in common, but each band resorted to the part of the country that was most accessible from their summer village. They did not always resort to the same places, but the whole country was thoroughly hunted over as often as once in two or three years. They started with little or no provisions, leaving behind them none but such as were unable to walk and could not be carried, and such of their relatives as stayed with the invalids to take care of them. Few were willing to be left behind, for the deer-hunt with all its hardships had strong attractions for young and old, and all were wanted. The old man or woman, who could do nothing else, could beguile the time of the long winter evenings by recounting the exploits of their youth or the deeds of the hunters or warriors of other times.

Generally hunting parties did not travel far in a day, for many were heavily laden and it required considerable time to pitch the tents and prepare for the night. The few who had horses laid their heaviest burdens on them. Some of them used pack saddles. More commonly two poles, twelve or fifteen feet long, were attached

to the horse, like the shafts of a wagon, one end of the poles dragging on the ground, and the other being supported by a strap passing over the saddle and drawn by another strap around the breast
of the horse like an ordinary breast-collar. Behind the horse was
a frame connecting the poles, on which the load was laid. Dogs
were harnessed in the same manner. This rude vehicle answered
their purpose well, both in summer and winter, and indeed they
often traveled where they could use no other. In passing the
streams, the rear end of the shafts was held up by two men.

Though they carried with them no superfluous baggage, many
were heavily laden, and, if the hunt was successful, the weight of
their burdens increased as they progressed. A family which owned
horses or to which many strong women belonged, got along with
comparative ease, for they had not only less to carry, but out-
stripped others on the road. Arriving first on the camping ground,
they could select the best place for their tent and secure the nearest
wood, tent-poles, etc., so that the hardest labor often fell on those
who were least able to perform it, a sad thing but common among
all nations. The feeble, and those who had small children and
none to help them, often fared very hardly. The tent alone was a
heavy burden, and there were many other things to carry, besides
such children as could not walk.

Sometimes a relative or neighbor would lend a helping hand,
and burdens were laid on all who were able to carry anything, if
nothing more than a puppy too young to walk. Elderly men frequently assisted in transporting the baggage, and I have seen young
men carrying heavy burdens to aid their wives; but young hunters
seldom carried anything save their traps and weapons, and indeed
when on the hunting grounds did not accompany the moving party,
having other work to do.

The movements of a hunting party were regulated by orders
issued by the chiefs, or, if no chief were present, by one of the
principal men of the party. These orders were given out after the
wishes of a majority of the party had been ascertained by consultation, and were commonly proclaimed by a herald in the morning or
evening, the only times when the hunters were likely to be all at
home. In this manner the time was appointed for moving the camp
and the place of the next encampment, the direction which the hunt

was to take the following day, and many other things of like nature.

If the weather was cold, young men were appointed by name to build a fire at which the hunters met about daybreak, and from which they went together to the place of hunting. That all might have an equal chance at the game, the place for hunting was appointed for each day, and boundaries were prescribed over which none might pass, unless there should occur a particular necessity for it, such for instance as pursuing a wounded deer. If any one passed the prescribed limits, he ran the risk of having his gun broken. Sibley once had his cap confiscated for such an offense.

After the country had been thoroughly hunted over for a radius of several miles around the camp, orders were given to move to another place, and these removals were not always agreeable operations. If there were fordable streams not frozen over, all must wade through them, except little children. I once accompanied a large party which crossed a swamp twenty or thirty rods wide, and in some places two or three feet in depth, the ice being almost but not quite strong enough to bear. There must have been much suffering, but there was no whining.

When the camp was to be removed, the hunters started out early in the morning and brought the game taken to the prearranged place of encampment. Some lucky ones might be there with venison before the moving party arrived. There was a strife among the young and ambitious women as to which should be first on the road. In a large party, as all followed the same track, those in front were far in advance of those in the rear. While the last had the best path, the first had other advantages which have been mentioned.

On arrival at the camping ground, there was much to be done and little time in which to do it. If the snow were deep and the cold intense, many of the party must suffer severely. Fires were built on the ground, and children were wrapped in skins and blankets, but could not be made comfortable till the tepees were pitched, so that many of them were often crying with cold and hunger. In the meantime the women had their hands full. The snow was to be removed and the ground to be leveled, if it was rough. This work must be done with a hoe, a difficult and tedious operation, when the ground is hard frozen and the mercury below zero, as the writer can well remember, though he helped to do it but once, nearly forty years ago.

Fourteen tepee poles were to be found and dragged often a considerable distance through the snow, making two or three heavy loads for a strong woman. The tent was then erected, and dry grass cut up from some swamp was brought and put all around the tent or tepee on the outside, for the Indian women would not bank their tents with snow lest it should melt and injure the tent. Hay was also strewn inside to spread the beds on, for the frozen ground was hard and cold. Then wood was brought for the fire, very dry for they burn no other. Last of all water was brought and hung over the fire to warm or cook the supper, which by this time was well earned if ever suppers are. There were always some who had all this work to do alone, but commonly there were two or more women or girls in the tent.

These journeys were exceedingly hard on the feeble, the sickly, and the mothers of young infants. Though the babe were but a day or two old, the mother must take it up and go along with the rest, for the party could not wait for them. The labors of women with very young infants were made as light as possible by their relatives; and sometimes the whole party waited a while for the sick and feeble, if there was hope of a speedy recovery. If they could not walk, they were carried.

Some will ask, "Why did not the men accompany the women and aid them in the severe labor of moving?" Some of them did, especially those who were too old to hunt well, and frequently a young man would assist his wife in carrying the baggage, if she could not get along without him; but in most cases the women preferred to have their husbands and sons off with the hunters, as that was considered the proper place for all who were fit for the chase. Often, if the men had accompanied the women on their journey, they must all have gone without their suppers.

As a general rule, it was necessary that the women should take charge of the baggage and leave the men unimpeded to search for game; but habit that is adopted from necessity may sometimes be continued when it is unnecessary. The white man sits idly by and sees his wife or mother laboring, perhaps beyond her strength, in cooking or washing for him, not because she does not need his aid.

nor because he is unable to help her, but because it is work to which he is unaccustomed. He does not put his hands in the wash-tub, because it is not his business; and the Indian hunter does not help his wife or mother carry her load, because it is not his business. Very likely the white woman needs help as much as the Indian woman, but her husband lets her do her own work; and because the Indian lets his wife do her own work, the white man calls him a brute.

Indian men certainly did not have proper regard for the comfort of their women, but while they were out on hunting expeditions, they did their full share of the labor. The customs that were adapted to the requirements of a hunter's life were the best for them, while they were hunters. The division of labor between the men and women was equitable and such as their occupation required. Sometimes it was the harder on one sex, sometimes on the other. They often remained encamped many days in the same place; and while the men were out almost every day, frequently from daylight till long after dark, the women had a comparatively easy time.

Deer hunting may seem to the amateur sportsman a delightful recreation; but all who have tried it will admit that it is a laborious occupation. The Indian often went out after deer with as much reluctance as the worn-out farm laborer feels when going to the harvest field, and only went because he must hunt or he and his family would starve. If he could have been always sure of success, hunting would have had more attractions for him, as Indians liked to kill game; but the hunter often went out knowing that it was probable he would walk all day and kill nothing. The writer once lived a month with an active and industrious woung man, who, though he hunted from morning to night almost every day, killed but one deer during the month. His father-in-law, an elderly man, though he always accompanied the hunters, brought in only what was killed by others. Hunters generally had better luck than that, but there were some in every large party who did not and could not kill game enough to supply the wants of their own families. They often returned after a hard and fruitless day's work disheartened and mortified.

It is a mistake to suppose that Dakota men were too lazy to carry burdens. They did not commonly carry the baggage, but many of them did a great deal more carrying in the course of a year than the women did. They carried their traps and packages of furs long distances, and almost all the game was brought in by them, frequently many miles. Occasionally when men were over-loaded, they left a part of their venison where it was killed, or on the way home, and it was brought in by the women; but commonly the women had nothing to do with the game till it was laid down at the door, and it was no great hardship to cook it in their fashion. It was no uncommon thing for wounded deer to lead the hunters far away from the camp, and, if they were finally killed, they had to carry them many miles in the night, through rough regions, with-out roads, often slipping and stumbling under their burdens. Some-times the hunters received injuries in this way which resulted in death. The men also carried the sick and brought in the dead who died far from home.

The white visitors to an Indian village, seeing the women carry-ing wood a few rods, wrote down for the information of the public that the lazy men compelled their wives to carry all the burdens; but while the woman was carrying the wood, her husband perhaps, after a weary day spent in pursuing game, was bringing it home on his back a distance of five or ten miles. When the Dakota women were told that the men made them do all the work, they laughed for they knew better. They did much that is not considered ap-propriate work for civilized women, but there was little that would be considered appropriate work for white women to do.

The Dakotas did not admit that any one had a right to appro-priate the whole deer to himself because he killed it. Their rules required that any one who was hunting with others should, on killing a deer, give notice to any who were within hearing, by a certain shout, the meaning of which was well known, as it was only used on such occasions. Having given the signal, the hunter waited a while, and if no one came he cut up the deer and carried it home; but if one came the flesh was equally divided between the two, the one who killed the deer taking the skin. If two or three came, each had a right to a certain portion of the flesh, but only the three who were first to arrive had any claim to it. The one who killed the deer always kept the skin and wrapped up his part of the flesh in it.

These rules about the division of game were a great encouragement to the less skillful and less able hunters, for, if they killed
nothing themselves, they might hope not to return empty; and
the rules worked no injury to the more successful, for the families
must all be fed, and this plan saved them the labor of carrying the
meat home for others. There were few, however, who were always
so successful that they did not sometimes gladly avail themselves of
the privilege which the custom gave them; and the man who, when
young, scorned to carry home what another had killed, might be
glad to do it when he was old.

The entrails were commonly cooked and eaten on the spot where
the animal was killed. After the tripe had lain a few minutes on
the coals, the inside peeled off and it was as clean as though it had
been soaked in water the traditional nine days. But the Dakotas
were not very particular about cleaning the entrails more than they
could do with their knives, for they held that, as deer ate nothing
unclean, there could be no danger of defilement in eating them.
The stomach of a hunter, who perhaps has eaten nothing since the
day before, is not very fastidious, especially if the weather be cold.
It is said that the buffalo hunters ate some parts of that animal
raw; but the Medawakantonwan ate no raw flesh, not even when
dried.

After the hunters went out in the morning, the children in
the camp watched for their return with game. When a deer was
brought in, they all shouted Oo-koo-hoo! Oo-koo-hoo! making the
camp ring; and when they saw who had the skin, they yelled out
his name so loud that all in the tepees could hear. The children
continued to watch and proclaim the names of the successful hunters until it was too dark for them to be recognized, so that while
daylight lasted any one sitting in his tepee could know what game
had been killed and who had killed it. They had a variety of
shouts, each indicating some particular kind of animal, such as
deer, bear, elk, etc.

Frequently some of the hunters did not get in till very late
at night, and sometimes not till the next day, having pursued game
too far to return. They often started out in the morning without
eating, and, if they killed nothing, fasted all day. When food was
plenty the fast was broken in the evening, which was spent in feast-

ing and recounting the adventures of the day, or in listening to some old man while he told them of remarkable things which happened in the days of his youth, or in days long gone by. Young and old, filling the tepee, would listen with fixed and eager attention, while he related all the particulars of some disastrous or successful hunt or battle.

While hunting deer they came across many other kinds of game. Occasionally they found many bears, and always some raccoons, of which latter they were so fond that, instead of saving the skin for the traders, they often ate it with the rest of the animal, burning off the fur as the French Canadians do the hair from swine. Dogs were also singed and not skinned. The boys hunted rabbits and other small animals. Some of the men carried traps, and were on the lookout for otter and other fur animals. Fishers they baited with fresh meat, dragging it long distances on the snow, and caught them in wooden traps of their own manufacture.

When they saw a fresh track of a deer leading into a cluster of bushes, they did not at once follow it in, but first ran around the bushes, and, if no track led out, they then advanced toward the deer, which, having seen the hunters pass around it, lay still until they approached very near. This kind of hunting suited the old men who could not run much; but some of their hunting required a great deal of hard running, too hard for any but the young.

Many were sometimes hunting together, and if deer were plentiful the hunters seemed to be in great danger of being killed by each other, since they were often concealed by the oak shrubs among which the deer sought shelter in the winter. Rarely a hunter was thus killed, but fatal accidents seldom occurred, for they were so experienced, skillful, and cautious in the use of fire-arms, that when sober they were seldom injured by the careless or accidental discharge of their guns. They were not only quick to see whatever was within range of their guns, but also any object which might turn the ball from its intended direction. Being in such constant use of fire-arms, of course some of them were accidentally shot, and others might be injured by the accidental bursting of a gun; but in the hands of a sober Indian a gun seldom did more mischief than he intended.

If the hunters obtained a surplus of food on the way out, they left it protected by wooden pens to be taken up on their return. They usually returned from the winter hunt some time in January, many of the deer having by that time become quite lean. All the venison that was not needed for the present use had been cut in thin slices and dried over the fire, and all the tallow had been saved to eat with corn, rice, etc., if they had any; for, after all that has been said about the improvidence of the Indians, each family was anxious to save all the food possible for future use. Sometimes when there was food enough in the house, the whole family went without a meal, the lady of the house, in anticipation of fresh supplies, having dried and stored away all the meat on hand, and being unwilling to draw on her reserve stores. Of this fact the writer is a competent witness, having himself participated in the inconvenience occasioned by it.

Indeed, the experience of a few months residence with the Dakotas, in their own tepees, opened my eyes to many things that I should not otherwise have seen. Among other things that were new to me, I learned that they kept about as good a lookout for the future as their mode of life would admit. Nothing was wasted. All surplus food, whether animal or vegetable, was carefully preserved and kept in store for future contingencies. Roots and berries, fish and venison, were carefully dried and laid up against a time of need. Every old rag of clothing was converted to some useful purpose. Moccasins and all other articles of clothing were carefully repaired and made to last as long as possible; and while we were declaiming against the improvident habits of the Indians, they were astonished at our wastefulness.

When they returned from the deer-hunt, if they had been successful, they had heavy loads to bring back. If their luck had been very good, they had more than they could carry at once, and, carrying part of it forward a short distance, they left it and went back for the remainder. They were never sorry to be overloaded with the spoils of the chase, and the men, now having no more hunting to do, helped the women bring in the products of the hunt.

If the hunt proved a failure, as it sometimes did, they had little to carry home. On the upper Minnesota river, hunting parties in winter were sometimes so destitute of provisions that they ate their horses, if they had any, and numbers of the Indians perished on their way home.

Arriving at their village site, they pitched their tents in the shelter of some wood, and, as little could be done at that season of the year except fishing, they spent the time mostly in resting and visiting until the first of March. During this time they handed over their furs and such deer skins as they could spare to the traders, and, if they had corn or rice, dug it up to eat with their tallow. The women had considerable labor to perform, such as getting wood, dressing deer skins, making moccasins, etc., but the men had little to do. It was with them all, perhaps, the easiest time of the year, though if the hunt had proved unproductive it was on the other hand the hardest.

The interval of rest was improved in visiting relatives in other bands, and also their acquaintances in other villages. There was often a good deal of gambling, but they were tolerably quiet; for at that time they obtained little or no whiskey, and their camps presented no such scenes of wild disorder as were frequent among them in later years.

SUGAR MAKING AND FUR HUNTING.

The season of rest and recreation mentioned in the preceding chapter soon passed by, for it only lasted till March, when it was necessary to prepare for the muskrat-hunt and sugar-making. These two operations could not be carried on by the same persons at the same time, because the maple trees and muskrats were too far apart. Therefore they divided their forces, and some of the Indians made sugar while others hunted furs. A few of the women accompanied the men to the hunting ground, and a few of the men staid with the women at the sugar-bush; but the men were the fur-hunters, and the women were the sugar-makers.

Little need be said about the process of sugar making, as it was substantially the same as with us. In tapping the trees they cut holes in them with axes, and they caught the sap in little troughs made of square pieces of birch bark bent to the right shape and held by a few stitches at each end. When the season was over, the pieces of bark were straightened and buried in the earth, to be used again. Their sugar was kept in covered baskets, made of birch bark. The sugar making and the preparation for it required most of the time in March and April. They who have made maple sugar know that although it is pleasant to the taste, it is not very pleasant work to make it; and it was especially disagreeable to those whose feet had no protection from the melting snow except buckskin moccasins.

In the mean time the hunters were off to the haunts of the muskrats, for they had promised a certain number of their skins to the trader, and if they failed to make their promise good he might not trust them again. The spring hunt was the most important, for the furs were then the most valuable. There were a few muskrats in all parts of the country, but they were not everywhere plentiful, and the Indians residing in the vicinity of Fort Snelling often went more than a hundred miles in quest of them, hunting south and west of Fort Ridgely. They were under the necessity of starting from home early in March, as it took some time to make the journey and the hunt commenced before the ice was out of the lakes. They usually carried a small supply of provisions, if they had any, also their guns, spears, and traps. Some had horses, but most carried their loads on their backs. They took some large traps for otter, and the muskrat traps were much heavier than those in use at the present day. These, with other necessary articles, made heavy burdens for men to carry a hundred miles.

It is well known that muskrats make houses in shallow lakes and marshes, constructing them of water plants cemented with mud. These houses resemble in size and shape a common cock of hay. The room in which the rats live is just above water, and sometimes is only large enough for one, but generally is made to accommodate several inmates. The covering of the houses is thick, and when frozen it is a defense against man and beast; but, on account of their dark color, the houses thaw out before the ice melts on the lakes in the spring, and as soon as they are thawed the hunt begins.

The muskrat spear is made of iron, three-fourths of an inch in diameter, and about three feet long, sharpened and barbed at the point, and is furnished with a wooden handle about three feet long. Armed with this, the hunter cautiously approached a rat house and thrust in the spear. If he had transfixed one or more, he cut open the house with his hatchet and took out the game.

When the ice disappeared, the muskrats were hunted with traps and guns. As they are in the habit of climbing on the tops of their houses, traps were often set on them and in doing this canoes were used. The muskrats move about more by night than by day, and industrious hunters spent a great part of the night in visiting their traps. Some of the canoes used for this purpose were so very small and light that it required great skill and experience to keep them right side up.

An Indian of my acquaintance related to me the particulars of an accident which happened to him while he was trapping in the night. He visited a trap which he had set on a rat house in a lake, when it was too dark for him to see it distinctly, and had the fingers of one hand caught in it. It was a strong trap with a spring at each end, but he could have opened it in an instant if he had been on land where he could use his feet. His situation as he sat on the water in his little canoe was rather embarrassing and soon became alarming, for, in attempting to free his hand, he only succeeded in getting the toes of one foot caught in the other end of the trap. He was now worse off than before, for he could not get on the top of the rat house and dared not move his little canoe lest he should fall into the water. He could not open the trap, as it had two springs and he but one hand. After considering a while, he took off his girdle and tied one end to the foot that was free, wound the girdle around one spring of the trap, and took the other end in his teeth. He then pressed down that spring with his hand and held it by drawing the belt tight with his foot and teeth, while he loosened the other spring.

Many of the muskrats were shot as they were swimming in the lakes and streams, especially by twilight. The Indians left most of their tents at home, so that not many of the fur-hunters were well housed. Provisions, too, were often scarce. In the winter and early spring the flesh of the muskrats was esteemed good eating; but when the warm weather drew on, muskrats were neither palatable nor wholesome, and those who ate them complained that they caused sore lips and other disorders.

As the Dakotas had no way of ascertaining the exact time of the year, they often thought the spring was nearer than it was, and consequently, in their haste to be on the hunting-grounds in season, arrived there too soon. Even if they had known the exact date in the year, they could not know just when the muskrat houses would thaw out, and they sometimes found themselves there with little or no provisions before either rats or ducks were to be had. When the ducks and geese arrived, they might have, but did not always have, plenty of wholesome food.

In 1836, I visited the fur hunters south of the site of Fort Ridgely, and found them living chiefly on muskrats. They themselves pronounced them unfit to be eaten. The weather was warm, the carcasses of the slaughtered animals lying everywhere in heaps, and the musky perfume, though good in its kind, was quite too much of a good thing. For want of anything better to eat, I gave the muskrats a fair trial, and perfectly agreed with the Indians in regard to their edible qualities; but when I asked them why, since ducks and geese were so plenty, they did not shoot some of them, they replied: "We came here to hunt furs, and have neither time nor ammunition to spend on other game." The fur season would soon be over, and, after going so far for furs, each wanted to secure his full quota of skins.

They generally returned in May, and, though they carried heavy loads out, they brought heavier ones back. If near the river, they made canoes and carried their burdens home by water. When they returned from the fur-hunt and sugar-camps, they resorted to their villages, and folding up their tents, entered their bark houses.

By this time they were destitute of provisions, what they had saved in winter being all consumed, and though they might not pray each day for their daily bread, they had to work for it daily. It is true that there were ducks on the water and fish in the water, but ducks are shy and have wings, and fish are not always as hungry as the fisherman and they bite only when they please. Whoever has tried hunting knows that wild birds and wild beasts are wary, and when much hunted they learn to take pretty good care of themselves. It was no light task to secure enough of them to furnish six or seven thousand of the Dakotas of Minnesota with their daily rations.

All the ground within many miles of the villages was soon hunted over, and the hunter who would find game must take a long walk for it. There was a well beaten path leading to each lake within reach far and near, and the fishermen did not suffer the grass to grow in them. They prowled around the margin of every lake and marsh, and no tortoise could venture on the land, or turtle put his head above the water, without running the risk of being captured.

Go where you would, you could hardly get out of sight of Indians, for they were to be seen always and everywhere in quest of something to eat. Their daily supplies of food must be obtained, and had been obtained no one knows how long, and the very fact that the Indians lived proved that they were a hard working race. They, if ever a people did, earned their living by hard labor. They had no property that brought gain to the owner while he rested, no income but that brought in daily by their own hands.

To them it was a perpetual, unceasing struggle for existence, and had been so throughout their past history. There never could have been a time when their very existence did not depend upon their active and unremitted exertions. In the meantime much else was to be done besides searching for the daily supplies of food. Fields, if they had any, were to be planted and cultivated, and houses to be built or repaired. The bark with which their houses were covered was in large pieces, thick, and very heavy when green. This bark they often carried several miles on their backs. Their fields were only little patches of ground, but they laid out a great deal of labor upon them. As soon as the corn was hoed, many of them left their bark houses and went off in quest of food, for by this time there was little game left in the vicinity of their villages.

Frequently in summer parties of men went off a day's journey or more to hunt, staying several days and drying their venison if they killed deer. They went also long distances after geese in moulting time. The Lake Calhoun band, while waiting for their corn to ripen, frequently lived a while chiefly on bullpouts which they caught by night in Mud Lake, a short distance above the "Little Waterfall," as the Dakotas called it, now Minnehaha, a name neither known nor understood by them.

SUMMER OCCUPATIONS.

In the summer the bands divided into small parties, each party going where it was hoped food would be found most abundant, or in pursuit of some article used for food or otherwise, which could be best procured at that season of the year. Some went after birch bark, to make sap troughs and sugar boxes for the next season; others went up the Mississippi, to pick blueberries; and some to the woods, to gather the stalks of the wild spikenard and other edible plants. Occasionally, some of the men went to the red pipestone quarry and brought home pieces of the stone for pipes. Indeed, they made excursions in all directions, and for various purposes.

Their eyes were on all kinds of fruit, watching the ripening process. Berries of all kinds were industriously gathered. In a word, they diligently sought out everything edible, whether it grew on bushes or trees, on the ground, or in the mud at the bottom of the lakes. While some were digging all day on the prairies for a peck of wild turnips, others were in the water up to their arms, exploring the bottom of the lakes in search of psinchincha. Nothing was so hidden that they did not find it, nor so hard to come at that they did not get it.

At all times of the year there were, besides clothing, many articles to be manufactured. Almost everything that they used in the way of implements, except those made of iron and steel, they made themselves; and, as they had few tools to work with, the process of manufacturing was slow and laborious. They had to smooth their timber without planes, cut it off without saws, and bore holes in it without augers.

Their mode of gathering corn has been described. When that was harvested, it was time to make preparations for the fall hunt, because the cold weather was coming on, and they would soon need a fresh supply of clothing, ammunition, etc. It must be strong cloth indeed that could long endure the wear and tear to which it was exposed on a Dakota man or woman. The hunter took little thought of his raiment as he crouched in the swamps, lying in wait for ducks, or rushed through the bushes in pursuit of game; and the garments of the women were also necessarily subjected to very rough usage. The blanket not only served for a cloak by day and a bed by night, but it was a general receptacle into which everything was gathered, and in which everything that needed to be put into a bag was transported. No article of clothing could last long with them, but must be often replaced. New guns, new kettles, etc., were also needed, as well as clothing and ammunition; and all these things must be paid for in furs, for there was no other currency.

How well so ever they were supplied in the spring, they might be destitute in the fall, for they bartered many of the goods received from traders with the Indians living farther west, for tents, robes, horses, etc.

They started on the fur hunt in September, and, as they left some in the spring to make sugar, so in the fall many went to the rice-lakes and cranberry-swamps. The seeds of the rice were easily shaken out by the wind, and therefore some went before it was ripe and tied the heads together in bunches. It is considerable labor to gather and clean wild rice, and though it is as abundant now as ever, probably none but Indians would think it worth harvesting. Some men who did not go for furs and many women picked cranberries, often carrying them long distances on their backs. Most of these they sold.

The fall fur-hunt frequently encroached on the deer-hunt. When the hunters returned from the haunts of the muskrats, it was high time to be off for the deer.

The foregoing is no exaggerated account of the yearly labors of the Dakotas, before they sold any portion of their lands. After they began to receive annuities, there was a rapid change in their habits, not for the better; but of that later time I am not writing. They are here described as they were when they supported themselves by hunting, and not as they were in that false position in which the policy of our government placed them, treating them more like paupers than like hunters or farmers. Hunting was the legitimate occupation of the uncivilized Dakota, and it was on the hunting-grounds that his good qualities were best exhibited. They who only saw him lounging listlessly about his tent, knew little about him. There was a great deal of hardihood, fortitude, foresight, and energy in a genuine Dakota; and it will be well for Minnesota if she never nourishes a race of men and women who have less native force of character and resolute determination than her aboriginal inhabitants.

WARLIKE PURSUITS.

In describing the employment of the Dakotas for the year, I have spoken only of their peaceful pursuits. In the midst of their other engagements, some of them found time to pay considerable attention to their neighbors, the Sacs, Pottawattamies, and especially the Ojibways, who indeed required a good deal of attention.

The Dakotas were not averse to undertaking these excursions against their hereditary enemies, and if they had been so peacefully inclined as not to go in search of them, their restless and warlike neighbors would have made work for them at home. The Indians did not make war on each other because they were Indians, but because they were men and like other men. Their wars were as necessary as wars generally are. If they were to live at all, they must have a country to live in; and if they were to live by hunting, they must have a very large country, from which all others were excluded. Such a country they had, not because their enemies were willing they should occupy it, but because they were able and determined to defend it by force of arms. If they had not resisted the encroachments of their enemies, they would soon have been deprived of the means of subsistence and must have perished. If they would have game to kill, they must kill men too.

The Ojibways boasted of having deprived them of a part of their country, and these Sioux were determined to keep them off from the remainder. In regard to the responsibility for these wars, we are not to suppose that the Dakotas or Sioux were more or less to blame than their neighbors. The Indians were none of them Quakers in principle or practice, and if they had from conscientious scruples been less averse to war we should have stronger proof than now that they did not belong to our race. Their propensity for fighting, and their love of military glory, furnished at least one indication and proof of their relationship to us. Here we meet on common ground, and those who had most signalized themselves in war were treated with the highest consideration by their civilized neighbors.

We might suppose that, whatever necessity there was originally for the prosecution of these hostilities, there could be none after Fort Snelling was built and the country placed under the protection of our troops. After we had a military force stationed at the

fort, there was for a time a cessation of hostilities between the
Dakotas and Ojibways who were near, but there was neither peace
nor truce between the Dakotas and Ojibways of Leech Lake and
Red Lake; and those who lived near the fort soon learned that
each must take care of himself. The garrison at Fort Snelling
protected just so much of the country as was enclosed within its
walls. Twice the Ojibways killed Dakotas within sight of the
fort, and they might have killed them with impunity right under
the portholes.

It was not possible for our government to compel each tribe
to respect the rights of others and hunt only on their own lands.
Long after Fort Snelling was built, the Dakotas sometimes found,
on going to their hunting grounds, that they had been anticipated
by the Ojibways, and that their game was all gone. It was of no
use to appeal in such cases to the commander of the garrison. It
would have been absurd for him to attempt to call Hole-in-the-Day
or the Pillagers of Leech Lake to account for game killed on the
lands of the Dakotas, for they would have laughed him to scorn.
The death of one intruder, shot down by the Dakotas, had more
salutary warning in it than all the admonitions that could be given
by the agent and military officers; and the Ojibways had more
respect for a little war party of Dakotas, skulking in the grass,
than for all the troops ever quartered at Fort Snelling.

Besides the necessity of defending their country, they had many
relatives killed by the enemy, whose death they felt bound in honor
to revenge.

It has been said that, in prosecuting their wars, they were actu-
ated less by patriotic motives than by a desire to show their prowess
and decorate their heads with eagle feathers. This may be all too
true, but patriotic motives alone are not always a sufficient stimulus
even for civilized soldiers. Certainly Indians are not the only
people ambitious of renown and eager in the pursuit of martial
fame. Civilized soldiers do not take scalps, nor adorn their heads
with eagle feathers, and we may hope they are all more or less
patriotic, but do not some of them keep at least one eye fixed on
epaulettes and stars and crosses of honor? What are medals and
badges of honor, and names of battle-fields inscribed on banners,
but substitutes for the eagle plumes of the Dakotas?

"But they were cruel, and their wars were attended with horrible barbarities." This is also true, for they were savages, and their cruelty is not to be justified or excused; but were Indians more cruel than other savage nations? If we would judge the Dakota with fairness, we must compare him not with nations who have enjoyed the benefits conferred by civilization and Christianity during thirty or forty generations, but with other savages; not with the Anglo-Saxons of the present day, but with the ancient Britons, Gauls, and Germans, who lived two thousand years ago. It would be easy to show that the Dakotas were not more barbarous than our ancestors, but this subject will be noticed in another place.

The Dakotas were bad enough, and their faults need no exaggeration. They were far from being gentle, innocent, harmless creatures, pure until contaminated by the whites, and committing acts of violence only when provoked beyond endurance. Romantic and sentimental writers may amuse themselves, and may deceive the simple, by such fabulous descriptions of the Indian character; but the real Dakota never sat for the picture, and would not feel flattered by it. He would have repudiated the meek and amiable virtues ascribed to him, for he held them in no high esteem. He often compared himself to a wolf, an animal which he resembled much more than he did a hare or deer. The Dakotas had strong, turbulent passions, easily excited, and almost entirely without the restraint of religious motives. We can only claim for them that they were by nature no worse than other men.

From what has been said in excuse of Dakota warfare, no one should infer that the writer would justify or palliate the atrocious massacre of the whites of Minnesota in 1862. The perpetrators of the horrible crimes then committed had been led onward to them by many years of luxurious idleness and riotous living. Hochokaduta, Little Crow, and their associates, had for more than twenty years been fed and clothed by government annuities. They had been furnished with tobacco to smoke, and money to buy whiskey; and all their wants had been so far supplied that they were enabled to spend a great portion of their time in idleness or something worse. The pressure of want being removed, the industrious habits of their ancestors were abandoned. As that restless energy which had characterized them found no legitimate fields of exercise it sought illegitimate ones, and they were fast losing every redeeming trait of savage character. In this state of demoralization they were gathered up and thrown together on their little Reserve, where all the worst characters could act in concert, and where they found bloody work for their idle hands to do.

Yet no one who knew them well can believe that in a deliberative assembly one out of ten of the Dakotas then on the Reserve, perhaps not ten among them all, would have been in favor of an attack on the whites. It was the work of a mob, begun by the few and carried on by the many, who were drawn into it by a great variety of motives. Some were influenced by that clannish feeling which prompted them, as it did the ancient Benjamites, to stand by their own people whether they were right or wrong. Some were intimidated by the insane violence of those who were drunk with blood. Many joined in the fight because they thought that, if the Dakotas were overcome, little discrimination would be made by the victors between the innocent and the guilty, a fear that came quite near enough to being realized. After all, a great many Indians on the Reserve held themselves aloof from deeds of violence, and did what they could for the preservation of the captives.

Whoever might be innocent or guilty of the massacre in 1862, the generation of which I am writing, and those who had preceded, were not responsible for it. The chiefs who visited Washington in 1837 were all dead excepting one, who was then an old man and out of office. He sat down and wept over the ruin which he could not prevent. None of that generation had imbrued their hands in the blood of white men. Major Taliaferro said that no white man was killed by a Dakota while he was in office as the agent from 1819 to 1840, and so much could not be said with truth of any of the neighboring tribes. The feet of the Dakotas were swift to shed the blood of their foes, but at the period of which I am writing they were friendly to the whites.

Tried by that standard by which alone they should be tried by their fellowmen, they were a manly race, with very prominent traits of character, both good and evil. They lived savages and most of them died savages, but while their sepulchers are with us let us not do injustice to their memories. Let us not wrong them, least of all while standing on their graves. They were not models for imitation, neither were they properly objects of contempt.

Whether their wars with their equally warlike neighbors were necessary or not, they were prosecuted with ceaseless vigilance and untiring energy. From the time when the snow disappeared in the spring till it fell again in the autumn, most of the time that could be spared from other avocations was improved or wasted by the young men in searching for their enemies. If they became remiss in this respect, they were likely to be reminded of their negligence by an unwelcome visit from their hostile neighbors. The inhabitants of a village would be suddenly startled by the simultaneous discharge of two or three or more guns; and, before they had time to rally, the triumphant foe was off with the scalp of one or more of their number beyond the reach of pursuit.

There were always insults to be resented, and injuries to be revenged; and if they would find the authors of these insults and injuries, they must seek them in the swamps and forests of their enemies' country. Long and toilsome journeys were made every summer far beyond their own frontiers, and as they dared not kill game or kindle fires in the vicinity of the enemy, they lurked around, carefully concealing themselves in grass or bushes, wet with dew and drenched by every shower, till some unlucky victim came within their reach, or, what was more often the case, till their provisions were exhausted and they were compelled to return home without scalps.

They said the Ojibways had greatly the advantage over them, because they could float down the current of the Mississippi, bringing plenty of provisions in their canoes, and being fresh and fit for action on their arrival. On the other hand, they were obliged, when invading the Ojibway country, to make long and toilsome marches on foot, carrying their weapons and provisions, and were exhausted when they most needed to be rested and refreshed.

A chief who had been a successful warrior in his youth, once told the writer that no man was brave when suffering for want of food and worn out by hard marching. It is not strange that they should have been sometimes a little faint-hearted, when they were fatigued and far from home and knew that if they struck a blow at the enemy they would be forced to a hasty retreat, followed by foes familiar with the country, swift of foot and thirsting for blood. The war parties were generally small and composed chiefly of very young men, while most of the men were engaged in other pursuits.

INDUSTRY OF THE HUNTER AND FARMER COMPARED.

I have been thus particular in describing the employments of the Dakotas in order to show that they had something else to do beesides lounging about in their wigwams, basking in the sunshine in summer, and sitting by the fire in winter.

It is true that they did not always hunt every day as steadily as the farmer goes about his daily labor, but some of the labors of the chase are too exhausting to be performed by any ordinary man without intermission. They frequently demand the most violent and long continued exertion, and hunters often returned so exhausted and lame that they needed several days to rest and recruit. Whoever saw them only during their intervals of rest might regard them as indolent fellows who never did anything. The Dakotas indeed were not all industrious, or else some of them were greatly slandered by their neighbors. There were too many loafers among them, but such persons were not in good repute and were not considered eligible husbands or sons-in-law.

Industry and enterprise were nowhere more highly prized than among the Dakotas, and a lazy man or woman was regarded as a public nuisance, for if one did not work others must work the harder. It is natural that white men who know little about the Dakotas, when they see many of them unwilling to engage in agricultural labors, should regard them as lazy, good-for-nothing fellows. But in regard to such labors they felt, as many a white man feels, disinclined to them and unfit for them. Many white men, having been educated for mercantile or professional business, and accustomed to no other, would be as unwilling to engage in hard labor on the farm or in the workshop, and would prove as inefficient there, as an Indian; and yet perhaps some of these very persons, who are both unable and unwilling to mow a swath or plow a furrow, and who, when thrown out of their ordinary employments, are a burden to their friends, declaim against Indian indolence and inefficiency.

The Dakota was a hunter, descended from a long line of hunters, trained to hunting by precept and example, with all the wisdom of a hunter that could be handed down by tradition or gained by experience, and with all the instincts of a hunter that could be transmitted by inheritance. Hence it is not strange that it is so difficult to make anything else of him.

To expect him to change at once all his habits, to become a steady, plodding farmer, is as absurd as it would be to expect that his dog, whose ancestors have been trained to hunt deer through a hundred generations, should be suddenly transformed into a docile shepherd dog, and should faithfully guard the flocks of his master.

GOVERNMENT.

The government of the Dakotas was purely democratic, the people holding all the powers of government in their own hands, and never delegating them to others except temporarily and for a special purpose. They claimed and exercised the right of deciding all questions which concerned the public interest. Their decisions were made in councils, frequently after long and animated debates, and sometimes not until after several successive meetings.

The decision was according to the will of the majority; but they seldom, if ever, attempted to carry out a measure by the use of violent means when the parties for and against it were nearly equal in numbers. If, when a measure was proposed in council, there was a general response of "Yes," the ayes had it and the measure was adopted; but if there was a general silence or a feeble response, it was lost.

Usually it was not necessary to appoint any officers to carry out the decision of the councils, for there was a general acquiescence and seldom any resistance. In ordinary cases all that was necessary was for the chief to make public proclamation of the doings of the council; but if any were refractory and refused to submit to the authority of the council, a number of active, resolute men were appointed to enforce the decrees. The men appointed to enforce laws commonly acted with promptness and decision.

My brother, Gideon H. Pond, once cut hay near the village at Oak Grove, and the tops of many of the stacks were deranged by the Indian children playing on them, so that the water penetrated them and the hay was spoiled. The next year he called together the most active and energetic of the boys, and, giving each a present of ammunition, he told them they were appointed soldiers to guard the hay. They accepted the office of special constable without hesitation, and watched the stacks with so much vigilance that none of them were injured. Some of these boys had been ringleaders in mischief the year before, but they knew what was expected from a soldier and discharged their duties faithfully.

When it became necessary to appoint officers to carry out a council decision, generally a sufficient number were appointed to overcome all anticipated resistance. On their way to punish a transgressor, they raised a certain shout, called the "officer's shout." which indicated that they were acting by public authority. They were authorized to break the guns, cut in pieces the clothing and tents of offenders, and, in extreme cases, to take their lives.

The Dakotas had no permanent officers except the chief and the chief soldier, and these officers had no authority except what was granted from time to time for special purposes. When the chief was about to transact public business with the officers of our government, he was advised what to do, and, if practicable, many of his people accompanied him to see that he observed his instructions.

If chiefs were induced to sign treaties without consulting their people, they were dissatisfied and were suspicious of unfair dealings; for they never permitted a chief or any other officer to act for them in public matters without their advice. An ignorance or a disregard of the democratic character of Indian government has been the source of much evil to them and to others; and they have often been accused of violating treaties which they felt under no obligation to observe.

As a general rule the office of chief was considered hereditary, but there were many disputes about the succession, and the office was sometimes seized by some other relative of the chief to the exclusion of his son. The rivalry between the competitors for the office was often so violent as to lead to bloodshed. This happened at Swan Lake, Carver, and Kaposia. Little Crow was wounded and two of his brothers were killed in a quarrel of this kind.

There was no difference in the rank of chiefs except that formerly some deference was paid to Wabashaw of Kiuksa, in consideration of signal services once rendered to the nation by one of his ancestors.

Besides the chief, there was in each band an officer called by the whites the "chief soldier." His office was considered inferior to that of the chief, but his personal qualities might give him greater authority with the band than the chief had. There was apt to be a jealousy between the chief and the chief soldier, a part of the band favoring one, and a part the other.

There had been a time in the history of the Dakotas when their chiefs were much fewer in number, and they were probably then of more importance in their official relation to their bands. They had very little influence in 1834. At that time many of them owed all their importance to the fact that the government transacted business with the Indians only through their chiefs. The necessity of having a chief at every little village, while it increased the number of the chiefs, diminished their influence.

Our government considered the chiefs competent to make contracts, binding on others; but no such power was delegated to them by their people. A chief might sign a treaty conveying away millions of acres of land, who would not have been employed by his people to make a contract for them to the amount of ten dollars.

At home the chiefs had no authority and little influence merely by virtue of their official position. They had no power to make laws themselves, nor were they entrusted with the execution of the laws made by others. They were seldom leaders of war parties, and were compelled to support themselves and their families just as others did. They were not ordinarily distinguished from the common people by any peculiar privileges, honors, or emoluments, except what they gained by their own merits.

Their power over their people depended chiefly upon their ability as speakers. If they could not make effective speeches, they were little heeded; but if they could speak well, they exercised great control over their respective bands.

They seldom or never attempted to carry out any important public measure in opposition to the wishes of a majority of their people. A chief might issue orders with a show of authority, but not before having first ascertained whether his orders were likely to be popular. The opinion of the people concerning any matter of public interest was commonly ascertained in a council, called for that purpose, where anyone could speak his sentiments; and in these popular assemblies there were often other men who had more influence than the chiefs.

LAWS.

The Dakotas had no authoritative enactments such as would be called laws among civilized people. They had customs which it was infamous to disregard, like that which has been mentioned concerning the division of the carcass of the deer. There were a great many of these traditionary rules which were generally observed, but the breach of these rules was seldom punished except by an expression of disapprobation. This popular odium was not, however, a light thing for an Indian to bear, for he could not isolate himself but must live continuously with those who upbraided and despised him.

Their temporary laws have been mentioned. They were frequently enacted, sometimes rigidly enforced, and might continue in operation many months at a time.

Most things that are considered great crimes by us were emphatically condemned by the Dakotas, and this was doubtless a great restraint to the evil-minded, preventing the commission of many crimes; but the guilty, though condemned by public opinion, were not punished by public authority.

Even murderers escaped punishment unless the relatives or friends of the murdered person avenged his death. Yet the fear of private retaliation afforded a better security for human life than one would expect. Each one knew that if he killed a person who had relatives able to avenge his death, he would probably have to answer for it with his own blood. He could not hope to escape through any technicality of the law, or by the disagreement of the jury. There was no place where he could hide himself and thus elude the avenger of blood, so that those who had relatives or friends able to avenge them were probably as safe as they would have been, among such a people, under the protection of law. They who had none to avenge them might be killed with impunity, but those who killed them were stigmatized as murderers, and their crimes were never forgotten.

The right to avenge the death of relatives was carried so far that some who had killed others accidentally were compelled tc redeem their lives with costly presents; but in all cases of that kind which fell under the observation of the writer, there was some suspicion that the manslaughter was not accidental. When one was killed in a sudden quarrel and the murder was not premeditated, the difficulty might be compromised without the death of the manslayer. Life was safer than one would suppose that it could be among such a people; but there were some who, like Joab, had committed more than one murder with impunity.

Other offences against individuals were punished. if punished at all, by individual or private retaliation.

The husband might punish his wife for unfaithfulness by cutting off the end of her nose, thus spoiling her beauty and rendering her less attractive to her paramours. Cases must have been rare in which women were thus treated, for the writer can recollect only two or three who were mutilated in the manner named. When the Dakotas were first visited by the white people, women were found among them who had been thus punished for adultery. It is a curious coincidence that some American sailors, who were recently shipwrecked on the northeast coast of Asia and spent a year or two among the natives of that region, report that women of that country who are unfaithful to their husbands are punished in this same manner.

Some crimes, such as theft, killing horses, etc., can hardly be said to have been punished at all, though their commission sometimes caused quarrels and provoked retaliation. They made few efforts to detect thieves, and were not much in the habit of reclaiming stolen property unless it was of considerable value. When they found property that had been stolen from them in the possession of others, they often said nothing and let the thieves enjoy it in peace.

PERSONAL APPEARANCE.

In stature the Dakotas are rather taller than people of European ancestry, that is, their average height appears to be greater. As they are a homogeneous people, there is more uniformity of stature among them than among white Americans. Not many are very tall or very short. Some of the women are tall and slender, but most of them are much shorter and stouter than the men.

The complexion of the Dakotas is considerably darker than of Europeans, but is not very dark. Their cheek bones are not particularly prominent, their features are regular, and many of them are good looking. Taken together the race cannot be characterized as a homely race.

The men are supposed to have little or no beards, but they must have taken much pains to extirpate them. Among those who have abandoned the custom of their forefathers, some whose faces were formerly as smooth as a woman's now wear respectable beards, to the surprise of their old acquaintances.

But little need be said about the size, features, complexion, etc., of the Dakotas, for these will probably continue to be what they now are for generations to come. The object of this work is not to tell what they are and will be, but what they have been and will never be again.

NATURAL DISPOSITION.

In regard to the natural temper and disposition of the Dakotas, there was the same diversity among them as among white people. Each individual had his own peculiarities, differing often very much from the peculiarities of others, so that a true description of one might be false when applied to another. Some were frank, communicative, and confiding; others were reserved, sly, and suspicious. Some were very good-natured, jovial and full of fun, while others were morose, and very seldom in a good humor; and between these two extremes, were all the different gradations of character. Yet they might, as a people, be characterized as agreeable and pleasant in temper and manners.

Many of them were entertaining in conversation, full of wit, good sense, and good humor, with a great relish for jokes and quick at repartee; while a few of them seemed to be almost always in a surly mood, and their conversation dull and disagreeable. They could not be called a taciturn people, for they loved to converse; but they had a quiet manner of speaking, and though often animated in conversation, were seldom rude or boisterous. They could, however, when they pleased, express themselves in terms far from mild and gentle, and make use of severe denunciation, keen sarcasm, and bitter irony. To carry some point with a white man, they would sometimes pretend to feel very much abused and offended; but if the trick was detected and they were told that their assumed indignation was all a mere pretence, they would often change their manner at once, and perhaps burst out into hearty laughter.

In mental abilities there was the same variety as among our own people. In respect to acquired knowledge, they were of course more on a level than are the members of a civilized community, where some are learned and some unlearned, for all had nearly equal advantages of education; but there was a great difference in their mental capacities, apparent to others and recognized by themselves. Some were bright and intelligent, quick of apprehension, and with tenacious memories; while others were stupid, their powers of perception dull, and their ideas few and confused.

It may be said of the Dakotas that they have good common sense. They were quick to distinguish between sound argument and sophistry, and many of them could reason with clearness, precision, and force. They were very close observers of men and things. Nothing visible escaped their notice, and they were peculiarly quick to discern the true character of their casual acquaintances. They soon found out all the strong points and all the weak points of a white man with whom they had to deal, and commonly knew a great deal more about him than he did about them.

They were very sensitive to ridicule, and had a great dread of appearing in a ludicrous light. It did not always please them to have white visitors, especially strangers, enter their homes, ask impertinent questions, and scan too closely their clothing, furniture, etc. They were too courteous to resent what they considered the impertinence of their ill-bred visitors, but they did not speak very flatteringly of them after they were gone, and it was unpleasant for one who knew their feelings to accompany such visitors to their tents and interpret for them.

In their intercourse with each other, they were, as a general thing, affable and courteous. The men seldom spoke to each other in loud, angry tones, even when their passions were greatly excited. When deadly enemies met, they often conversed with each other as pleasantly as though they had been the warmest friends. Their threats, when they intended to put them in execution, were uttered in a low voice and in ambiguous terms, less being said than was meant. Loud threats were intended only to alarm, and were addressed only to white men and children.

The women sometimes fought with each other with their hands, pulling hair, tearing garments, etc.; but sober men, in their quarrels with each other, seldom used any but deadly weapons. Angry scuffles and fighting with the fist were hardly known among them. An Indian, when sober, seldom struck his antagonist unless he intended to kill him. They concealed their anger unless greatly enraged, but it was dangerous to provoke them too far. A salutary fear of the knife, which was always at hand, doubtless made them more respectful and courteous in their deportment toward each other than they would have been without it. They did not, however, always suppress their angry emotions, and were seldom at a loss for words to express the most violent emotions or passions. The tongue was the weapon with which the women generally fought, and some of them knew very well how to wield it.

The Dakotas were not remarkable for retentive memories, either in regard to injuries received or favors bestowed on them. Certainly they did not retain a lasting and grateful remembrance of the benefits conferred on them, neither were their memories remarkably retentive of injuries. If they did not avenge an injury soon after it was inflicted, it commonly went unavenged; and no one acquainted with them counted much on their gratitude.

They were not very confiding, but, when they became thoroughly convinced that a man was honest, they would trust him with almost anything.

VICES AND CRIMES.

When the Dakotas were sober, murders were not very common among them. Some were killed, as already stated, while contending for the office of chief, and some on other occasions; but murders committed by sober men were rare among the Medawakantonwan, and not very frequent among the upper Indians. Most of the murders were committed by men, very few by women. Generally when a murder was committed, there was no attempt to conceal it, and no difficulty in discovering the murderers.

Suicide was very rare among the men, but common among women. Many years ago a man shot himself at Lac qui Parle, some said accidentally, others said intentionally; and that is the only case of the alleged suicide of a Dakota man that the writer now recalls. The women destroyed themselves for various reasons, but generally when in a furious passion. Some committed suicide because they were despondent and weary of life; some to avoid marrying men whom they disliked, as was the case with two of Little Crow's sisters. A woman at Lac qui Parle killed herself because her husband had cut gashes in her face to punish her for adultery.

Some killed themselves because they were angry and thought their death would cause grief to those who had offended them. Women and girls frequently threatened to kill themselves, and probably some of them were treated better than they would have been if there had been no fear that the threat would be executed. Suicides almost always hanged themselves with the strap used in carrying bundles; but tradition tells of one who leaped from a precipice on the east side of Lake Pepin, and of another who went over the Falls of St. Anthony. During my residence among the Dakotas, I found two women hanging by the neck, just in time to save their lives.

Drunkenness, as it prevailed among the Dakotas, was terrible in its effects, producing in many cases temporary insanity. They were not tipplers, but either abstained from drinking ardent spirits or drank to intoxication. They did not seem to have any desire to drink intoxicating drinks in moderate quantities, or in solitude, though in later times some of them told me they were trying to learn to drink without getting drunk, like white men. They liked to drink in company and to have enough whiskey to make all drunk. Their revels on these occasions probably bore a close resemblance to the carousals of the old Scandinavians and other nations of northern Europe.

Not long after drinking began, all were drunk together, though in different stages of inebriation. The whiskey produced very different effects on different individuals. All were noisy and talkative, but not all in the same frame of mind. Some were good-natured, silly, and harmless, while others were raging like wild beasts. Some were in high spirits and very merry, while others were wailing as if their hearts would break, and calling by name upon their friends who were dead. Though the liquor was dealt out in equal quantities to all, its effects on the bodies of the drinkers were as diverse as on their minds. While some were soon overcome by it and helpless, others seemed more active and strong when drunk than when sober.

These individual peculiarities were exhibited so uniformly, that their acquaintances soon learned who were to be feared and who not; and those known to be most dangerous were securely bound as soon as possible after they began to drink. If the men were all drunk, the work of binding the unruly fell on the women. It was a hard task, but they were strong and generally succeeded in performing it. Drunken men, however, were often permitted to run loose, causing great consternation among the women and children, and sometimes doing great harm.

I never saw a young Dakota woman drunk, while living among her own people; and many of the middle-aged and old women abstained entirely from drinking whiskey, but some were drunkards. As a general rule the women were sober, as were also some of the young men. It was difficult for the men to refuse an invitation to a feast or drinking bout, but some of them would contrive to be out of the way when whiskey was on hand.

There was not much drunkenness among the Dakotas for several years before they sold their lands on the east side of the Mississippi, in 1837, and a person might be with them a year without seeing one of them drunk. They had been furnished with whiskey in earlier times, but at that period they could obtain none from the traders, and the enterprising pioneer merchants of St. Paul had not commenced their lucrative and destructive work among them. Though the Dakotas were so much addicted to the use of whiskey, they could abstain from its use when they pleased. Notorious drunkards could take heavy kegs of it on their backs at St. Paul, and, following circuitous routes to avoid the villages on their way, carry their burdens to Lac qui Parle, more than two hundred miles or even still farther, and finally barter them for horses, without tasting of the contents.

After whiskey became abundant here, General Sibley, the missionaries, and others, induced many of the Indians to pledge their word to abstain from drinking it. These pledges or promises were for limited periods, as for three months, six months, or a year, and were seldom broken, though the person who gave the pledge would perhaps be drunk the day after the time expired.

Adultery and kindred vices or crimes will be noticed elsewhere.

The thievish propensities of the Dakotas were pretty strong, and property was seldom safe when so exposed that they could take it with little danger of detection. Although they made a practice of stealing, theft was condemned and the habitual thief was despised; but it was deemed less disgraceful to pilfer from the whites than from their own people. As among the Spartans, the guilt of stealing was not so great in their estimation as the disgrace of being detected.

Not many of the Dakotas had a very strict regard for the truth; when under strong temptation to lie, few of them could be trusted. Ordinarily their statements could be relied upon, but were to be received with caution if they could gain anything by prevarication. In regard to integrity and truthfulness, there was a great difference among them. Some were esteemed as thieves and liars, and others were accounted honest and truthful.

Their standard of honesty was not altogether perfect, but they evidently did not believe that all were thieves. There were many against whom they did not think it necessary to be on the watch, also many who had a good reputation for veracity among their acquaintance. Theft and falsehood had no open advocates, and no one spoke well of notorious thieves and liars.

If one had been guilty of some misdemeanor, it was considered a mark of manliness for him to make a frank confession of his misdeeds. When mischief was done it was not often long before the author was discovered; for, though the Dakotas were artful dissemblers, they could not long keep a secret.

We certainly found them far from being a conscientious people, but in this we were not disappointed. Every one ought to know, without being told, that the honest, harmless, innocent heathen is an imaginary being, and does not belong to the human race.

LANGUAGE AND PICTURE WRITING.

The language of the Dakotas is not so imperfect as one would naturally expect among a people so rude and uncultivated. It is well adapted to their use, and is adequate to the expression of their ideas with force, conciseness, and precision. In its present state, it could not be used as the language of a civilized people, for it would require many additions before it could represent all the ideas that are readily expressed in any of the languages of Europe; but it is probably as susceptible of improvement as those languages were when spoken by savages. One who is master of the Dakota can find no difficulty in saying whatever he wishes concerning such things as engaged the attention of the uncivilized Dakotas. The language is easy of acquisition to those who begin to learn it in childhood, for it has few irregularities and its system of vowel sounds is very simple indeed. It is very difficult, however, for adult persons to learn to speak it well, because it has many sounds not readily perceived by ears unaccustomed to them nor easily uttered by organs of speech not trained from childhood. Most of these sounds can not be described, for they are not found in European languages and can be taught only by the voice.

The Dakotas had a system of calls or shouts, which were of great service when they wished to communicate information to those who were too far off to understand articulate words. The shout which gave notice of the killing of a deer has been mentioned, also the "soldier's shout" raised by those who were about to execute the decree of a council. One was a signal of alarm, giving notice that the enemy was near. When this was heard it was passed instantly from one to another, warning all to avoid the danger or to prepare for defense. The different shouts or warnings could never be misunderstood, and their signification was instantly recognized.

Besides these, there were signals which conveyed information as far as they could be seen, being generally made by waving the blanket. They had also a very extensive system of gestures, well understood by all, which enabled them to carry on considerable conversation in dumb show. This was of great use especially when they were lying in ambush and dared not speak. The gestures were often used when there was no necssity for them, so that by practice they became very expert.

They occasionally made use of picture-writing, drawing figures on bark or on a tree that had been peeled, and could in this way convey to others considerable information. Once, with an old man and his son, I passed through a village where we found no one at home, and the old man, who was a chief, wished to leave his card. His name was Eagle Head, and with charcoal he drew on a board the figure of a man with the head of an eagle. He then drew the picture of a man with a hat on and one without. The addition of two guns and a dog completed the description of our party. The direction of our faces showed which way we were going. All was done in a minute, for no pains were taken to draw correct likenesses.

ORATORY.

Speeches well made and well timed had a great influence. over the minds of the Dakotas, and a few words fitly spoken often changed the purposes of the inhabitants of a whole village. The influence and authority of a chief depended almost entirely on his abilities as a speaker, for no force was used to compel obedience to his commands. However highly esteemed a chief might be for upright conduct, if he was not a ready speaker he was little regarded; while a bad man, if he could make a good speech, exercised great control over his men.

Shapaydan (Shakopee), who was for more than thirty years chief of a large band at Shakopee, by his superior abilities as a speaker always maintained an ascendancy over his people, although on some accounts he was very much disliked by many of them. Some other chiefs, who were much more highly esteemed for their probity than he, could not restrain their bands or lead them as they wished, because they were not eloquent speakers. I have heard Dakotas say that if Shakopee had been alive in 1862, there would have been no rising of the Indians against the whites.

Eloquence being of so much importance, it was natural that those who aspired to be leaders of the people should cultivate the art of speaking; but they spent no time in learning to assume striking attitudes, or to make graceful or impressive gestures. They were speakers, not actors, and addressed themselves to the ear, not to the eye.

It is true that the Indians frequently make use of gestures, both in private conversation and in public speaking; and a popular writer has said that their language is so imperfect that they cannot make themselves understood by words alone, but he was mistaken. When they spoke in a tepee in council, they sat in a circle on the ground, wrapped in their blankets, with their hands clasped around their knees, and each speaker sat still in his place. A Dakota once said to the writer, "Do white men hear with their eyes? I notice they keep them fixed on the speaker."

Often when a chief made a speech he was seen by few or none of his auditors, for they were in their tepees and he stood out of doors. Frequently no one knew that he intended to speak till they heard his voice. When he began to speak, conversation ceased and all listened till the speech was ended. Then, if it was approved, there was a general response of "Yes." Dissent was expressed by silence.

I have heard Shakopee make many speeches in the night, between two villages which were forty rods apart. In winter most of the speeches were made after dark at night or before daylight in the morning, night being the only time when the men were all at home. Whether by night or by day, they were addressed to unseen audiences, the hearers being in their tepees and the speaker outside.

Of course speeches were often made to the people while they were standing or sitting around the speaker in the open air. Doubtless many of the most effective speeches were made under such circumstances, but even then those who listened attentively were more likely to have their eyes fixed on the ground than on the speaker.·

Dakota speeches were, as might be expected, more remarkable for spirit and force than for smoothness and elegance. Their orators were not all necessarily rude in speech, for none could be more plausible and insinuating in address than they; but they doubtless adopted that style because they found it productive of the greatest effect on the multitude. With all their rudeness, some of their harangues, if they had been properly translated, would be worth preserving.

Some of their poorest speeches were made when they were transacting business with the officers of our government, for their people were dissatisfied if they let such an occasion pass without soliciting presents, and their begging spoiled their speeches. If any of them happened to make a good speech at the agency house or fort, it would hardly be regarded as such after being rendered into English by a careless or incompetent interpreter.

Their best speeches were made to their own people, and were called out by some sudden emergency that caused great excitement. Such a speech was made by Little Six (Shapaydan) after the slaughter of the Ojibways on Rum river, where he had some men killed and many wounded. The Ojibway men, who had been absent hunting when their families were killed, were just coming in sight, and the speech was addressed to the Lake Calhoun men, who, he thought, were going to hurry off the field and leave him and his men alone with their wounded. The speech was short, but those to whom it was addressed were so impressed by it that they remembered and repeated portions of it after their return.

The best addresses of Indian orators must have been made under such circumstances that few white men were likely to hear them or to hear of them. They were delivered at some critical moment, when good counsel was urgently needed, and when there was no time for premeditation or deliberation. The eloquent speaker who was not found wanting on such occasions was justly esteemed a public benefactor, and stood high in the estimation of the people.

When making set speeches on ordinary occasions, the speaker often commenced in a rambling manner, passing from topic to topic, with much circumlocution slowly approaching the main subject of discourse. At other times, the business in hand was introduced at once with great abruptness. It was necessary for them to speak very loud in order to be heard by the people in their tepees; and in addressing white men in set speeches they often spoke much louder than was necessary. It was so difficult to give a literal rendering of their speeches in English that the interpreters seldom attempted to give anything more than the substance of them, and if the Dakotas had understood English they would hardly have recognized their own speeches.

In almost all translations of Indian speeches that have been published, the speakers are represented as repeating their own names instead of using pronouns when referring to themselves. That certainly is not the practice with the Dakotas, who would be much less likely to use proper names in that way than would a white man.

POETRY.

The Dakotas had little that could be called poetry. There was nothing in the language, composed by them, that could properly be called a poem or a song. They had popular tunes, some of which were probably very ancient, but no songs except a very few words which were occasionally repeated when the tunes were sung.

The following words were sung at a scalp dance: "He stood pointing his gun, but missed fire, and I was not afraid." This is a fair specimen of their songs, if they can be called such. Sometimes a mourner would extemporize a few words while wailing for the dead, but even that was rare. None seemed to have any idea of composing what could be termed poetry. I once received from the half-blood, Scott Campbell, some pieces of composition that purported to be Dakota songs, but the Indians did not recognize them.

If the Dakotas had any poetry it was not in songs but in fables, of which they had a great store. Some of their fables bear marks of high antiquity, as in them no allusion is made to fire-arms, nor to anything received from white men, while varieties of trees and plants are mentioned which are abundant farther north, but not common in this part of the country. Many of the stories are the product of an inventive genius and active imagination, and need only the right form of words to make them poems. They constitute the poetry of this people.

These fables are full of the supernatural and are made up of many strange events and wild adventures, but they will hardly bear a literal translation into English, and to civilize is to spoil them.

Years ago the Dakotas were in the habit of repeating these tales for the entertainment of company, and I have known a crowd to fill a tepee and listen with fixed attention to the recital for hours during the long winter evenings.

MUSIC AND MUSICAL INSTRUMENTS.

Mention has been made of their popular tunes, and there were many of these, each appropriated to some special service. Probably some of them had been sung by them and their ancestors for many generations.

One of these tunes was used by mourners, and that and no other was used by them all in wailing for the dead. One was used to express feelings of terror and dismay. This is what we call the "death-song," but the Dakotas called it "the song or tune of terror," and it was sung when they were in great peril. It was reported of the delegation of chiefs which went to Washington in 1837, that some of them began to sing this tune when without any warning they were carried into a railroad tunnel; and this is the tune that was sung on the scaffold by those who were hung at Mankato.

Another of these tunes was sung when the recipient of a present made a public acknowledgment of the generosity of the donor, and yet another when they were gambling with the ball and moccasin. Each dance and religious feast had its appropriate tune. There are a great many of these tunes and they were sung very frequently, so that, although few have a less discriminating ear for music than the writer, he learned to distinguish them, and when singing was heard in the camp he knew at once what was going on by the tune that was sung. A few words were occasionally sung with these tunes, as a sort of chorus; but they were sung a great deal without any words at all.

It would be presumption in me to attempt to criticise Dakota music. I can only say of their singing that it seemed to me to accord well with the character of the singers. The loud, wild notes were doubtless animating to their spirits and pleasing to their ears, but not to mine.

Some of their singing, especially when heard in the night, had a weird, unearthly sound. The loud, rude voices of the singers, and the dismal sound of the drum, made music that accorded well with the war-whoop of the young braves, the wailing of mourners, and the howling of conjurers, all of which might be heard at the same time.

The musical instruments most used were the drum, rattle, and flute. The drum was made by straining parchment, made of deer-skin, over the end of a powder keg. Probably in earlier times a piece of hollow log was used. This drum was beaten in a very monotonous manner with a single stick. The sound was dull and not particularly inspiring, but could be heard quite a distance. Light portable drums were made by putting parchment heads on hoops, five or six inches broad, and fifteen or eighteen inches in diameter.

The rattle was made of a gourd shell, into which were put the round teeth of the white bass. This instrument was used principally by conjurers. They made other rattles of deer hoofs, or of pieces of metal attached to a handle, and these were used in some dances.

Flutes might be made of sumac, but by the Medawakantonwans they were commonly made of red cedar. A stick was first made of the requisite size and shape for the tube, then was split through the middle, and the two pieces were hollowed out and glued together again. The sounds produced by this little instrument were very agreeable; its soft melody, which was quite in contrast with their other music, proved that they had a relish for sounds less harsh than those produced by the drum and rattle. Often a young man might be seen sitting alone, playing on a flute of his own making, and seemingly delighted with its soft, sweet tones. That the women were pleased with the sounds of the flute may be inferred from the fact that it was much used in serenading young ladies.

NOTATION.

The Dakotas compute numbers like other people, by tens; because, like other people, they have ten fingers and thumbs on their hands. Their names for numbers are very much like our own. They count ten, two tens, three tens, etc., till they reach a hundred, then commence again, and when they have reached ten hundred, call it one thousand and begin again. In fact their mode of counting is substantially the same as our own. Their name for a million was coined for them by interpreters, when they sold their lands, and the most intelligent of them did not at first understand it, not having before had occasion to use it.

They count a great deal on their fingers, and often hold them up in answer to the question, How many? They practice this so much that many of them will straighten out what fingers they please, keeping the rest closed. The fingers may represent units, tens, hundreds, or thousands. If they wish to signify ten they hold open both hands; and if twenty, thirty, etc., they open and close the hands as many times as there are tens in the number.

Time was measured by days, or rather by nights, and by moons. None of the Dakotas knew the exact number of days in a year. One of them told the writer that he had tried to ascertain the number by cutting a notch in a stick for each day, but when the year came round he had no means of ascertaining the precise day on which he began to count.

Being very close and careful observers of natural phenomena, they could tell very nearly the time of the year in summer by the appearance of vegetation, and in winter by the fetuses of the animals which they killed, but of course the information obtained from such sources could not be exact. They seemed most at fault about the time of year in February and March, and looked anxiously for the return of the crows, who were the harbingers of spring and always brought welcome tidings to the Dakotas, for they knew that the ducks and geese were not far behind.

They had an absurd way of accounting for the wane of the moon, saying that it was eaten up. The moon-eater seemed quite unequal to the task assigned him, for he was nothing more than a little mouse of a peculiar form, a species found occasionally though rather rarely in this country. How much credence this queer fancy gained among the Dakotas is uncertain, for, when bantered about it, they laughed and did not seem to care whether it was true or not. They had no better way of accounting for the decrease of the moon, and perhaps their theory was as good as none. Lying outdoors so often by night, they learned to appreciate the value of the moon as a luminary and were unwilling that it should suffer harm.

While sleeping one night in one of their camps, I was suddenly aroused by the discharge of fire-arms. Running out to learn the cause, I found the moon eclipsed and the Indians trying to frighten away the monster which had assailed it. They succeeded in this praiseworthy attempt, as doubtless their ancestors had done for generations before them, and so would be encouraged to try it again when necessary.

They were close observers of the stars, and had given names to many single stars and constellations. In the absence of the moon, they looked at the stars as we do at a timepiece to learn the time at night.

STANDARDS OF MEASURE.

In measuring cloth the Dakotas used the distance from the ear to the end of the longest finger, turning the head so that the measure with a man of ordinary size was about a yard in length. Poles, canoes, etc., were measured by the fathom, the distance between the ends of the fingers when both arms are extended in opposite directions. For short measures they used the span and the hand's breadth.

In pacing distances they did not walk as we do, taking long steps, but put the feet as far apart as possible. This was a laborious way of measuring and was used only for short distances. Long distances were measured by day's journeys or a part of a day's journey. Some young men once measured the distance from Kaposia to Mendota, and from Mendota to Lake Calhoun, by bow shots, but probably this mode of measurement was not often resorted to.

They had no standard for weights and liquid measures, and none for dry measure except the hands.

RELIGION AND WORSHIP.

It is not easy to exhibit the religious views of the Dakotas in a very clear or satisfactory light. Their external forms of worship can be described, but I shall not attempt to tell just what they thought of things unseen, for many of their notions concerning supernatural things were confused, unsettled, and contradictory.

I went among them with a determination to know all that was to be learned about them, and especially about their views on religious subjects. For this purpose I carefully observed all that was to be seen of their acts of worship, even entering their wakan feasts and taking part in their ceremonies. All the information that was to be gained by conversing with the most intelligent and communicative among them convinced me, after a careful research, extending through many years, during which I made a diligent use of my eyes and ears, that they had no fixed, uniform belief.

Probably a harmonious system of mythology was never found among any heathen people. Each pagan writer, when speaking of the gods, would aim to be consistent with himself, but these writers do not always harmonize with each other; and the superstitious notions of the common people were perhaps as confused and contradictory as those of the American Indians. The great poets of pagan Greece and Rome were great inventors, and they sometimes drew on their invention or imagination much more than Milton did in writing his "Paradise Lost."

My brother, Gideon H. Pond, in a little work published some years ago, has perhaps done as much to reduce this discordant and chaotic mass of materials to order as any one can; but I will tell some things about their superstitious notions and practices, because this work would be incomplete were no such statement included. His paper, entitled "Dakota Superstitions and Dakota Gods," forms pages 215-255 in the second volume of the Minnesota Historical Society Collections. Another paper, on "The Religion of the Dakotas," by James W. Lynd, is in pages 150-174 of the same volume.

The Dakotas had certain ideas about religious subjects which were not taught them by their prophets and had no connection with their superstitions, but which seem to have been the suggestion of reason and conscience. These ideas were deficient rather than erroneous, but mention of them will be made in another place. Here I am speaking of their superstitions, the inventions of their wakan-men. No well-informed person will expect to find in the mythology of the Dakotas a well defined system. As they had no books and no class of persons whose business it was to teach the common people the articles of religious belief, each one knew only what he happened to hear, and some heard one thing and some another.

If the members of the Wakan-lodge had any knowledge of these things more than others, they kept such knowledge to themselves; but it is probable that if all their secrets had been divulged, they would have amounted to nothing more than crafty devices for upholding the credit of their own order.

The religion of the Dakotas consisted principally, but not wholly, in the worship of visible things of this world, animate and inanimate. Their chief object of worship was Unkteri, the mammoth, though they held many erroneous opinions concerning that extinct species of elephant, and did not know that the race was extinct. They had seen bones of the mammoth, pieces of which they had in their possession, and they were too well acquainted with comparative anatomy not to know that it was a quadruped. They described the species as resembling the buffalo or ox, but of enormous size. As they worshipped many other animals, it was natural that the mammoth, which so much exceeded the others in size, should be adopted as their chief god. To his worship their most solemn religious festivals were dedicated. They supposed that the race was still in existence, and, as they were not seen on land and their bones were found in low and wet places, they concluded that their dwelling was in the water. Their bones were highly prized for magical powers, and were perhaps as valuable to them as relics of a saint are to a devout Catholic. A Dakota told me that he had discovered some of the fossil bones in the lake opposite Shakopee, but was unable to raise them without some boat larger than a canoe.

The Dakotas supposed that thunder was the voice of a bird, which used lightning as a means of destroying enemies. Many of them really thought they had seen this marvelous bird. With a prior belief in its existence, it is not strange that a terrified imagination should discover it among the dark flying clouds of a thunder storm. This bird they worshipped.

Another object of worship was Taku-Shkan-Shkan, or that which moves. Stones were the symbol of this deity, and, sometimes at least, his dwelling-place. The Indians believed that some stones possessed the power of locomotion, or were moved by some invisible, supernatural power; and intelligent men affirmed that they had seen stones which had moved some distance on level ground, leaving a track or furrow behind them. The moving of the stone and the track behind it were doubtless the work of some cunning rogue, but some men of good common sense evidently believed that some stones could move or were moved by the god of which they were the symbol.

Many prayers were addressed to ghosts, who were never very far away, and, if the Indians did not see them, they often heard them whistle, especially in the night. That affection of the muscles of the face, by which the features are distorted and the mouth drawn to one side, was supposed to be the work of ghosts. They had the same fear of the spirits of the dead that many white persons have, and kept out of their way as much as possible, but often worshipped them.

The sun and moon were worshipped to some extent by the Dakotas about the sources of the Minnesota river, but rarely by the Medawakantonwan.

Heyoka, also called Waziya, was an imaginary being of gigantic size, with sensations opposite to those felt by mortals; that is, in winter he was oppressed by heat, and in summer suffered with cold, or was sad when he should be merry, and was merry when he should be sad. He was doubtless the invention of some fertile genius, ambitious to astonish the people with something new and strange.

Unktomi was another of their fabulous beings, who, though seldom worshipped, was often spoken of and acted an important part in some of their fables. He was a notorious liar, and more noted for cunning than for honesty. To him was ascribed the manufacture of the stone arrowheads occasionally found in this country.

Both Heyoka and Unktomi were eccentric characters, and were not always spoken of with reverence. Their exploits were not unlike those of the fairies, brownies, and such ilk of other lands. Except perhaps Unktomi, all the individuals and objects which have been mentioned were worshipped by the Dakotas. There was hardly anything visible that some of them did not occasionally worship, but of such a being as the Creator and Preserver of all they had no knowledge.

In their intercourse with the whites, they had heard of a God and a devil. The former they called Wakantanka, and the latter Wakanshicha, commonly translated Great Spirit and Evil Spirit; but the Great Spirit was the God of the foreigners, to whom they owed no allegiance. When talking with a white man they might say, "The Great Spirit hears me," in confirmation of the truth of their statements; but to one of their own people they were more likely to say, "The earth hears me."

They were as a people very superstitious, and were often engaged in some act of worship to some one of their vast variety of gods. They called frequently upon ghosts without much formality. The hunter or traveler, stopping to smoke, would fill his pipe and holding it up would say, "Here, ghosts, take a smoke and give us a good day."

Stones were much worshipped by them, both with prayers and offerings. They chose granite boulders and painted them red. There was a large sacred stone of this sort at Red Rock, from which the place takes its name, and another between Kaposia and Mendota. Both were covered with votive offerings, such as tobacco, pieces of cloth, hatchets, knives, arrows, and other articles of small value.

They did not always speak of their gods with the greatest respect, and it was uncertain how much or how little confidence some of them had in them. The writer happened to be standing with Shakopee near some painted stone gods, when he spoke of them with the utmost contempt, and of their worshippers as silly fools; but he acknowledged that he would not venture to speak so before the Dakotas, and he appeared to be a zealous worshipper of such things as long as he lived.

I once traveled several days on foot with a chief, and when we encamped at night he made the figure of a turtle in the earth, and prayed to it for good weather. He seemed somewhat offended when I told him that his prayers would avail nothing, and stoutly maintained that it was not a vain thing to pray to turtles for good weather. The next day was fair, and he told me with an air of triumph that I could now see the efficacy of his prayers. Of course I had to yield the point, for facts are stronger than arguments.

At our next encampment, the first thing he did was to renew his devotions to the turtle. We needed fair weather, for it was early in April and we had no shelter, but this time the turtle failed to respond. In the night we were drenched by a cold rain. I suggested to the old man that it would be well for him to get up and call upon his god; but he was in a bad humor, spoke very disrespectfully of turtles, and declared he would be revenged on the next one he met. The disappointment, however, did not cure him of his idolatry; and he maintained that if I could not obtain fair weather by praying for it, my God was no better than his.

The chief of the Lake Calhoun band, a thoughtful man of good judgment, told me that he regarded many of the wakan-men as impostcrs, but that he thought some of them honest men and their statements concerning supernatural things reliable. Such was probably the opinion of many intelligent and thoughtful persons among them. The facts before narrated show that many of the Dakotas were unsettled in their minds, not being firm in their belief of all that was taught by their prophets.

The efforts made by the wakan-men to keep up their credit proved that there was much skepticism among the people, of which they were afraid. Indeed, there were few things concerning which the religious teachers were themselves agreed; and it is probable that their superstitious notions and ceremonies had from time to time been subject to many innovations, for there was nothing to prevent such changes.

It was claimed and generally believed that there were some in every generation to whom the gods revealed themselves. It was a common thing for individuals to assert that they had received special revelations from the unseen world; and there was so much confidence in the truth of these assertions, or the people were so much afraid to question their truth, that the movements of whole villages were governed by them.

At one time when the whooping-cough prevailed at Lake Calhoun, it was revealed to Red Bird, a noted conjurer, that if the whole band would follow him to the bank of the lake and smoke a certain pipe while he held it, the disease would depart. This ceremony was performed, women carrying their little children that they might take a whiff from the mysterious pipe, which doubtless conferred as much benefit as white children receive when the hands of a wonder-working doctor are laid on their heads. The prophet knew enough not to perform the ceremony until he perceived indubitable signs of an abatement of the disease, and he also knew enough to apply to the writer for medicine for his own children.

On another occasion I was with a hunting party when game was scarce, and it was revealed to one of the wise men that the ghosts of certain cattle which had been killed by some of the party were accompanying us and driving away the game. It was also made known that if all the company would go through a certain round of ceremonies, and then rush back in a body across a lake that we had passed, the ghosts would leave us. I was urged by the leader to join them in the phantom chase, because it was thought the shades of the cattle would have more regard for a white man than for Indians. After spending two or three days and nights in preliminary preparations, a part of which consisted in arraying themselves in fantastic and ludicrous apparel and making queer looking weapons, such as had been prescribed by the god who had been so kind as to tell us how to get rid of our invisible enemies, all the party, with great shouting, rushed back across the frozen lake, and we heard no more of the cattle. Whatever doubts any may have had concerning the efficacy of the remedy, they kept to themselves, but many appeared to regard it as a farce. The performance was well timed, as we were just entering a region where game was likely to be more plentiful.

The accounts here given are specimens of the special revelations made to the wakan-men, whenever they could turn them to their own advantage and gain credit with the people. The authority of these prophets was as great as that of any who had gone before, and why should they study the traditions of the past, when they themselves had direct access to the gods who were the fountains of light? Like our modern necromancers, they held direct communication with the invisible and spiritual world. There was a nearer way to gain knowledge of things supernatural than to attempt to gain it from the uncertain traditions of the past. At the same time these men could have very little reverence for the revelations made to others.

Truthfulness has required me to say hard things about wakan-men, and some of them were exceedingly mean; but many of them were good warriors and good hunters, kind to their families and staunch friends, with as much magnanimity and generosity as we could reasonably expect to find among savage pagans.

Like some of our own spiritualists, many wakan-men were not only very wicked but very shrewd, and as they knew that they themselves were impostors, they must at least have suspected that the prophets who went before them were false prophets like themselves. Religious forms and doctrines could have no certain and stable character in the hands of such men, but must necessarily be subject to mutations and full of contradictions. They were not so much the expounders of the doctrines of others as disseminators of their own fancies, and there were so many of them acting without concert, each seeking his own aggrandizement by the invention of falsehoods, that it would have been unreasonable to expect to find agreement and consistency among them.

It is natural for those who write about Indian superstitions to wish to furnish the public with some regular system of mythology. If they do not question too many of the wakan-men, they may think they have found what they are seeking for; but if they extend their researches too far, their system will all crumble to pieces, and they will find themselves surrounded by chaotic fragments. If anyone wishes to construct a consistent system of Indian mythology, such as will be satisfactory to the public, the best way for him to do it is to form a theory of his own, adopt some Indian notions, reject others, invent some himself, and not ask the Indians too many questions.

We have conclusive proof that the superstitious rites and ceremonies of the Dakotas did not continue unchangeably the same from generation to generation. The "medicine lodge," which occupied so conspicuous a place among the religious ceremonies of the Dakotas on the Mississippi and Minnesota rivers, is not found among the Ihanktonwan of the Missouri; but if it had been originally a Dakota institution, we should expect to find it among all the Dakota tribes. It is evident that at a time not very remote it was adopted by the eastern Dakotas, or was abandoned by their western relatives; and either its abandonment or adoption implies a great instability in their religious belief. If such an innovation was tolerated, then almost any change might take place in their religious views and practices.

Yet the Dakotas had a certain routine of religious ceremonies, some of which were doubtless very ancient and may have been little changed for generations. It is probable that in the main they worshipped the same objects which their ancestors had worshipped from time immemorial. With many of these acts of worship the wakan-men had no more to do than the common people, and they would have continued the same if there had been no wakan-men. Their religion consisted much in private acts of worship, which were too numerous and varied to be all described,

and which each performed or neglected according to his own inclination.

THE MEDICINE DANCE.

A brief account will here be given of some of the most common
forms of public worship, beginning with the wakan-dance, commonly called the "medicine dance." It has been mentioned that
the Wakan society or "medicine lodge" is not common to all the
Dakotas. The eastern Dakotas may have received it from their
neighbors, the Ojibways, Winnebagoes, Sacs, or Foxes, all of whom
had it. It is a sacred society, the free masonry of the Indians; and,
as the writer was never initiated into its mysteries, he will not
pretend to reveal its secrets.

In justice to the members of the society, it is perhaps proper
to say that they, like members of other secret societies, affirmed
that all that was done among them in secret was very good. Those
who were received into this society paid liberal fees for admission,
and received bags made of the entire skins of small animals or
birds, containing some little things which they were taught to
consider of great value. Besides the wakan-bag and its contents,
they received instruction and advice, which was said to be very
good; but probably the most that they learned was the proper
manner of performing the ceremonies and maintaining the credit
of the society. New bags were not always provided for the candidates, but such as had belonged to deceased members of the lodge
were given to their descendants or others. Some who applied for
admission were rejected, but for what reason I cannot tell, as
the lodge was composed of all sorts of persons, comprising in its
membership some of the worst and some of the best.

The ceremonies attending the wakan-dance were in part the
most imposing and in part the most absurd of any witnessed among
the Dakotas. This dance was not held very often, but generally
as often as two or three times each year at each village. There
seems to have been no rule requiring it to be celebrated always
when it was, for I have heard Dakotas complain at times that it
was held too often.

Much food was first collected as a preliminary, without which
nothing could be done. In the winter I have known them to
contribute the breasts of deer to one who gave notice that he intended to hold a dance in the spring.

A smooth, dry place was selected and inclosed by setting stakes around it four or five feet in height, and tents were then hung on the poles or stakes. The inclosure was eight or ten rods long and twenty or thirty feet wide, and the fence so low that the spectators could look over it. At one end of the inclosed space a large shelter was constructed by putting several tents together, so arranged that the side toward the dancing-ground was always open during the dance. This tent was the headquarters of the principal men and women, for the lodge was composed of both sexes in about equal numbers. It was occupied a day or two before the dance commenced, for the purpose of receiving candidates and performing such other occult services as were necessary.

When the day for the dance arrived, a number of large kettles, filled with choice food, were hung over a fire at the end of the enclosure, opposite the tent, and persons were appointed to attend to them during the day.

Before the dance began, most of the dancers arranged themselves in two rows or lines, one on each side of the inclosed area, with their backs to the fence, and holding their wakan-bags in their hands. They were without their blankets but arrayed in their best apparel, except the newly initiated, who, if they were males, were painted black and wore only their breech-cloths. Not a smile was to be seen on their faces, nor was a light word spoken by them during the performance.

The time was measured by a drum and vocal music, and in the intervals of the dance short speeches or invocations were made by some of the leaders. The ball was opened by a few, who passed down from the tent in front of one of the lines, crossed over near the kettles, and returned in front of the other line. They trotted rather than danced, taking short, quick steps, and bending forward. They held the wakan-bag or medicine-sack before them, grasping the neck in front with the right hand, the other end being held in the left hand close to the side of the performer, so that the head of the skin was held pointing forward. At every step each one uttered a sort of grunt, and their whole appearance while dancing formed a mixture of the hideous and ludicrous which might have been amusing if it had not been disgusting.

After the persons who led off the dance had passed up and down the lines a few times, they suddenly turned, one after another, and each touched on the breast, with the head of the bag, one of those who stood in the lines. The one who was touched, uttering a groan or shriek, fell suddenly on his or her face headlong on the ground, and, after lying apparently lifeless a minute or so, began slowly to recover, raised himself or herself a little on the hands, and succeeded, after several convulsive efforts, in coughing up a little shell or bean.

This person then arose, and after trotting around the circle a while, touched one who fell and did as he had done. Whenever one had shot down another, he took his place in line and stood still till he was shot again. The process of touching with the sack they termed "shooting."

In this way the dance could be kept up a great while, for when one was weary he had only to call out another and take his place among those who were resting. It was left to the option of each one to touch whom he pleased, and, as no one knew when his turn would come, all had to be ready to fall at any time. Some dropped as though they had been shot, but others, especially the older ones, were more careful of themselves in falling. It seemed strange that persons who had so keen a sense of the ludicrous, and such a dread of appearing ridiculous, could have been persuaded to make such an exhibition. Theirs, however, were not the only worshipping assemblies in which the solemn and ridiculous have been mingled together.

But the ludicrous part of the wakan-dance was not the worst of it. It was a deception or an attempt to deceive, for they would have the bystander believe that, when the bag touched them, the shell, or whatever it was, passed through their breasts into their bodies and was afterwards coughed up. They claimed that they did not fall voluntarily, but were shot down. Doubtless many of the spectators found it difficult to believe such palpable absurdities, but there was nothing to be gained by publishing their skeptical thoughts, for it was not a light thing to incur the displeasure of some of the wakan-men. If their incantations were harmless, their poisons were not, though they threatened to do more harm than they really did. Probably many of the dancers did not expect

that what was said about the shell would be universally received
as true, for when I ventured to banter some of them about it, their
only answer was a good-natured laugh.   As with the pagan nations
of ancient times, so with them, superstitions and recreations were
so mingled that it was difficult to separate them, and to tell when
they were serious and when in sport.

The dance, with short intervals of rest, was kept up from morning till near night, and then came the feast.   The food was of
the best they could procure, the dancers were hungry, and doubtless the feast was as acceptable to them as a royal banquet to
those who fare sumptuously every day.   The spectators looked on
with wishful eyes, and perhaps the sight of the feast, from which
they were excluded, induced some of them to become members of
the Wakan society for the sake of the good cheer.

These festivals were great occasions, often drawing together
nearly all the population of two or three villages.   The dancing-
ground was always surrounded by a host of spectators, who, aware
of the solemnity of the occasion, observed the strictest decorum.
In a later period whiskey was sometimes drunk at wakan-dances,
but the practice was severely reprehended by many of the Dakotas,
although perhaps it was not more incongruous and unseemly than
the Christmas carousals which some of them had opportunities of
observing among their white neighbors.

WAKAN FEASTS.

Less ceremonious wakan-feasts were very common, and might be
made by anyone at any time.   If food was plentiful, several feasts
of this kind might be in progress at the same time in a camp or
village.   When a man prepared to make a wakan-feast, the women
and children left the tent and staid in some neighboring tent till
it was over.   The food was divided as equally as possible into a
number of portions, corresponding to the number of guests to be
invited.   Each of these portions was usually as large as one could
conveniently eat at one time.   Several men were sent for to assist
in the ceremonies, and while the food was being cooked two or more
were engaged in praying, or rather wailing in loud recitative tones.
They called it praying, but the word to pray is derived from the
word weep, and in these feasts they wept rather than prayed.

The devotional exercises were continued most of the time while the food was being prepared.

When the feast was ready, a messenger went around and invited each of the guests in a low tone of voice. The one who was invited carried his own dish with him to the feast, where, after some preliminary ceremonies, such as fumigating the hands and knives with the smoke of cedar leaves, the master of the feast gave to each one a portion which he must eat up there and then or otherwise pay a forfeit. Generally the present given to the master of the feast by those who failed to devour the portion set before them was some such thing as a pair of leggings or cloth for a shirt. None of the food might be carried away, and the bones were carefully collected and thrown into the water. If the portions of food given at these feasts were unreasonably large, the guests complained of the imposition.

After the feast was ended, as the guests withdrew, each one. when he reached the door, turned and saluted all who were left in the tent, addressing each individually, and, if a relative, by the title indicating the relationship, as "my cousin," "my brother-in-law," etc. This parting salutation was a trying ordeal for some. and I have seen young and bashful women very much embarrassed on such occasions.

As already remarked, these feasts were very frequent. When they were killing deer in abundance many ate little except at wakan-feasts. The hunters, returning hungry from hunting, often abstained a while from eating, lest, after taking supper, they should be called to a feast and be unable to eat what was set before them. When hungry they were glad to be invited, but, when not hungry, I have known them to go very reluctantly and not without valid reason for their reluctance, because they must gorge themselves like boa constrictors or give some present which perhaps they could not well spare, as these were debts which they felt themselves under religious obligations to pay.

Food that was needed in the family was often lavishly expended in these feasts, sometimes when the owner would gladly have saved it for his own use if he could have done so without injury to his reputation, but he wished to be as generous as his neighbors and was ashamed to eat of their food while they never tasted of his. He wanted to make as good a show of ability as others, and, prompted by generosity or vanity, incurred greater expense often than his means would justify.

I once heard a discussion between a Dakota and his wife, concerning the expediency of making a feast. The man was in favor of it, but the woman demurred on the ground that they could not afford it. This the husband admitted, was true, but said that they had made no feast that winter, and had feasted with others without inviting them in return till he was ashamed to do it any longer. The mother-in-law voted for the feast, and it was made. Are such consultations ever heard except in the tents of the Dakotas?

They thought their success in hunting was greatest when they made wakan-feasts most frequently, which was probably true, but they may have mistaken the cause for the effect. It seems probable that they first made use of these supplications in times of great scarcity of provisions, and if their wants seemed to be supplied in answer to their prayers they would be likely to renew their supplications in all times of extremity, till they finally came to regard their frequent repetitions as essential to their welfare. The prayers in the wakan-feast were addressed to Unkteri, the mammoth, whose worship was noted on a preceding page.

It may not be improper here to notice that gluttony for which Indians have been notorious. The Dakotas, when actively employed, did not eat often and were in the habit of devouring large quantities of food at a time. They frequently hunted all day without eating, and, as already stated, it was not an uncommon thing for them to start out in the morning without breakfast and eat nothing till they returned at night. These long fasts were of course followed by hearty meals, and hunters' stomachs became so distended, by filling them to their utmost capacity, that they would contain enormous quantities of food. When a white man saw how much an Indian could devour at once, he set him down as a glutton. But, though he could and did eat so much at one time, his meals were often "few and far between."

He also needed more food in winter in consequence of being more exposed to the cold than we are. In cold weather, either by night or by day, the Dakota man or woman was seldom what we would call comfortably warm, and if they stepped into a warm room they were often so overcome by the heat as to fall asleep immediately. If they had not been hearty eaters, they would have succumbed to the cold.

They who eat only one kind of food at a time, prepared in the simplest manner, seem to eat larger quantities than those who have a variety at each meal. One accustomed to our mode of living, if compelled to live on fresh meat alone, will be surprised to learn how much it takes to satisfy him. Few white men can eat as much at a single meal as an ordinary Dakota, but let them live with the Indians, faring in all respects as they fared, and they would learn soon to rival them in eating.

White men who acccompanied the Dakota delegation to Washington in 1837 said that after the Indians had been fed a few days on the diet of white people, they ate no more than others; and one of the chiefs told me, after his return, that the food eaten by white men was much more hearty than the food of the Indians, so that a very little satisfied.

It was natural that a people whose supply of provisions was so precarious, and who had so few sources of enjoyment, should make the matter of eating so prominent as to produce an unfavorable impression on those who had never experienced a scarcity of food. Moreover, it is not strange that they who heard them talk so much about eating, and saw them eat so much at a time, should call them gluttons; but probably a much larger proportion of white persons than of Dakotas injure themselves by high living.

The Feast of Raw Fish.

This feast, if it could be so named, was celebrated only when it was revealed to some one that it was absolutely necessary, which was not very often, for the Dakotas were not fond of raw fish nor raw flesh of any kind. It required some time to prepare for this ceremony. The chief actors, those who devoured the fish, represented beasts and birds of prey. Some personated wolves, bears, foxes, etc.; and others hawks, cormorants, and other rapacious birds. Those who represented quadrupeds, finding their arms too short for legs, lengthened them by holding short sticks in their hands. Each assumed the appearance and imitated the manner, as well as he could, of the beast or bird which he represented. They also attempted to imitate their voices, and in this some of them succeeded very well; for it is a part of their craft, as hunters and warriors, to learn to mimic the voices of birds and beasts. Those who assumed the character of birds used pipes or whistles, made for the occasion.

At the only performance of this kind witnessed by the writer, they had two pike, weighing three or four pounds apiece, painted blue, and lying on the ground, inclosed by a slight fence. The beasts and birds walked about the pen, often approaching it as though anxious to get the fish, and as often starting back in alarm, until at last, a signal being given, they all pounced upon the fish. As beasts and birds have no hands, they devoured them without touching them with anything but their mouths. Their teeth were sharp and their jaws strong, and the fish soon disappeared, bones and all. There was less danger in swallowing the bones than there would have been had the fish been cooked, for the flesh adhered to them firmly and they were swallowed with it.

Any one, after reading this account, will be ready to conclude that the tastes of the Dakotas were brutish, and that their stomachs would revolt at nothing; but it was as beasts, not as men, that they ate the raw fish. They did it as a religious duty, to secure a benediction or avert a calamity; or perhaps some shared in the ceremony to show that they could do what others could do. Not one of the performers on that occasion could have been induced to swallow a raw oyster, or probably not even one that was cooked. I suppose they did not relish the dish set before them, for one of them slyly showed me a bitter herb which he put in his mouth just before the attack on the fish commenced. The Dakotas were not eaters of raw flesh, and if some of them did sometimes swallow bits of the flesh of their enemies, as was reported, it was done in a spirit of bravado, or in the madness of excitement. I have seen a Frenchman, when very hungry, eat the raw flesh of a muskrat; but he was sharply rebuked for it by a Dakota, and probably few of them would have done it except in case of absolute necessity.

About some kinds of food they seemed to be quite fastidious, refusing, for example, to eat dried beef until it was cooked. To eat raw oysters and dried herring, as many of the civilized do, would have been regarded by them as an abominable practice. There are a few eels in the Minnesota river, but the Indians, who called them snake fish, never learned to eat them.

As I was once passing through the village of Good Road, he called me into his house to help eat an eel. He said he had seen eels eaten in Washington, and knew they must be good. Some of his people had caught one, he had ordered it to be cooked, and was determined it should be eaten, but his men were afraid of it. He had invited them to the feast, but only a part of them had ventured to come. He divided the eel into as many parts as there were persons present, giving each a very small piece. The chief praised the eel, but waited for me to taste it first. He then ate his portion, and the others, one by one, swallowed what was given them, but with a very bad grace, and looking very much as if they were afraid they were eating a snake. I relate this anecdote in connection with the story of the raw fish, because I consider it unfair to present only the worst side of the Indian character.

HEYOKA FEAST.

Another feast was instituted in honor of the god Heyoka, to whom cold was as heat and heat as cold, etc. His votaries stood around a kettle of food, and, taking it out of the boiling water with their hands, ate it without waiting for it to cool. When the hot broth was sprinkled on their naked bodies, they shivered as if it had been cold water. They claimed to be, for the time, proof against the injurious effects of heat, and may have had some method of deadening the sensibilities of the skin; but their performances, as I have seen them, were not very marvelous and did not seem to excite much wonder in the minds of the spectators.

It is true that they snatched the meat from the boiling water, and ate it immediately; but they were quick and cautious in their motions, and snatched the food from each other before it had time to scald them so as to raise a blister, and if they did feel a little pain, they would not be likely to complain. When they sprinkled the broth on each other, they took the precaution to toss it high in the air. During the performance the spectators stood by, enjoying the sport, neither contradicting nor believing what was said by the fire-eaters. It was enough for them that the exhibition furnished amusement for an idle hour.

THE SUN DANCE.

As I never witnessed this dance, I shall not attempt to describe it. It is common among the Dakotas on the western plains, and has been minutely described by some who have seen it. It was sometimes performed by the Dakotas of the upper Minnesota river, but not often. The dancers danced with their faces toward the sun, till their strength was exhausted. They inserted sticks under the muscles of the arms or body, and, fastening one end of a cord to these sticks and the other end to a post or some heavy weight, pulled on them till the flesh gave way.

This was the only religious service among the Dakotas in which the devotees inflicted upon themselves severe bodily torture; and these painful and bloody rites were not popular with the Dakotas of the Mississippi and Minnesota.

They were willing to go through a weary round of ceremonies, to do any amount of praying and dancing in honor of their gods, provided a good feast at the end made amends for all their fatigue; but, except when mourning for the dead, they seldom afflicted themselves with bodily tortures, for neither their faith nor their zeal carried them so far as to make them willing to torment themselves to please either gods or men.

THUNDER DANCE.

The manner in which the Dakotas worshipped the Thunder bird, if it can be called worship, seemed rather designed to intimidate than to propitiate this god. Like all other sacred dances of the Dakotas, it was attended with many little whimsical ceremonies, too numerous to be minutely described. An image of the thunder bird was made and fastened to a pole twenty or thirty feet high, around which the worshippers, if they could be so designated, danced. At the close of the ceremonies, they shot at the pole near the top until they cut it in two with their bullets, when the likeness of the bird fell to the ground.

Occasionally some of the Dakotas were killed by lightning, and it was natural that they should wish to find out a remedy for the evil; but it does not seem reasonable to suppose the thunder bird would be more favorably disposed toward them after being treated thus in effigy.

A wakan-man, however, was wiser than seven men who can render a reason. If we would find good sense among any people, we must not look for it in their superstition, for that is always unreasonable, whether among the savage or the civilized.

MAKING A BEAR.

This performance, like many other things done by the Dakotas, seemed to partake of the nature both of a diversion and of a religious solemnity. The man who represented the bear constructed his den by digging a hole in the earth about two feet deep, with paths leading out from it toward each of the four cardinal points. The den was inclosed with a slight fence, and the bear stayed by it a day or two, going through a certain formula of ceremonies. To lengthen his arms so that he could walk on all fours, he carried hoops in his hands which he used as paws.

On the last day of the play a number of young men gathered around him, having their guns loaded with powder only. When they drew near the den, the bear rushed out and chased them, trying to catch them by clapping the hoops over their heads. This was repeated until he had been out by three of the paths which led from the hole. The fourth time he was chased by the hunters, who fired very near him till he fell, and the farce was ended.

THE ELK DANCE.

In this dance the men who performed were entirely naked, and were painted to resemble the elk. They danced in the evening, however, when it was too dark for them to be distinctly seen, or at least that was the case in all dances of the kind seen by me.

There were others of these semi-religious dances or plays; but perhaps enough and more than enough have been described.

THE VAPOR BATH.

In preparing for this bath, a small hemispherical framework was constructed by sticking the ends of slender poles in the ground and bending them over. The frame was covered with skins or blankets, being only three or four feet high, just large enough to accommodate those who were to undergo or enjoy the steaming. Water was poured on heated stones placed in this little tent, filling the interior instantly with hot vapor.

What particular ceremonies were connected with this bath, I do not know. It was considered a religious rite, and the same kind of stones were used as they were accustomed to worship, that is, waterworn cobblestones, about three or four pounds in weight.

Rev. J. P. Williamson tells me that the Dakotas who have professed to renounce idolatry seem more reluctant to abandon this than any other of their superstitious practices. They may retain the vapor bath less from superstitious motives than for the sake of the supposed beneficial influence upon the health. Hennepin, who was very ill when he came to the villages of the Dakotas near Mille Lacs, tells us that they at once prepared for him a vapor bath, and that apparently through its effects he regained his accustomed health and strength.

Sacrifices and Offerings.

The Dakotas were accustomed to make votive offerings. Generally these were of no great value. The small articles placed on the stones which they worshipped have been mentioned. Offerings were also made to other objects of worship, some offerings being thrown into the water, others laid on the ground, and yet others hung in the air.

Dogs were offered in sacrifice, and also game killed in hunting. After being killed, dogs were thrown into the water, or were marked with paint and left lying on the ground, sometimes covered with a piece of cloth or blanket.

They often hung on trees or poles offerings of cloth, blankets, or skins. These were generally new, and were left hanging until they decayed.

Such offerings were often made or promised when the parties making them were about to engage in some hazardous undertaking, and they were often made just before the departure of a war party or just after its return. I do not think they were ever offered as an expiation for sin. It was not easy to learn from them just what their views were about the object and efficacy of these oblations, as they did not converse freely concerning such things, at least not with white men, and probably not among themselves.

It is not improbable that they often thus invoked the aid of the gods in the prosecution of enterprises which they preferred to keep secret. The sacrifices and votive offerings belonged rather to private devotions than to public worship. They were frequently offered very privately, sometimes in sequestered places, and were seldom a subject of conversation. Doubtless they would have seemed very natural and proper to one of the ancient Greeks or Romans. They seemed to have very little connection with their more formal acts of public worship, and were probably more ancient than the latter.

JUGGLERY.

There were jugglers among the Dakotas, who, if the reports of eye-witnesses were true, were not a whit behind the wizards of other lands. They claimed to possess supernatural powers, and their claims were as well sustained by proofs as such claims are among any people. They were not spiritualists, but they either performed some of the same wonders by the help of their gods as the spiritualists do by the help of the spirits of the dead, or they practiced the same impositions on the people under one pretense as our spiritualists do under another. They knew how to release themselves when fast bound hand and foot with cords, and I heard of this exploit among the Dakotas before I heard of its being done anywhere else.

I have heard of many marvelous things done by Dakota jugglers, some of which were witnessed by white men of unquestionable veracity; but as I never witnessed them myself I shall not describe them.

SUPERSTITIONS.

The most prominent forms of worship prevalent among these aborigines have been described, but I have not noticed all the little ceremonies observed by them. No one can ever be perfectly acquainted with all the minutiæ of their superstition, who is not reared among them, and of many I am doubtless ignorant; but I have seen more than I feel inclined to describe, and perhaps have already written more than any one will be disposed to read.

The mythology of the Dakotas is a chaos of incoherent imaginations, a mass of palpable absurdities. We should be surprised to find people so intelligent and shrewd about many things entertaining such crude and ridiculous notions about religion, if such inconsistencies were peculiar to them. While the rude Dakota pleases his imaginary god by purifying his hands with the smoke of cedar leaves, the enlightened ritualist glorifies the Most High by shutting out the light of the sun and burning candles at noonday. One shakes his rattle, the other jingles his bells, and perhaps the noise of the rattle is as acceptable to God as the sound of the bells.

Many of the religious formalities of the Dakotas seemed to be without end or aim, and some of them whimsical and ludicrous; but they had many maxims, enforced by religious motives, the object of which was evident and laudable.

Many things were forbidden on the ground that they were wakan, that is, the doing of them would be followed by some calamity. It was as dangerous to do them as it once was for our ancestors, and perhaps still is for some of our contemporaries, to begin an important undertaking on Friday. To declare a thing wakan was often nothing more than an attempt to prevent improper or dangerous things from being done by an appeal to superstitious fears. Thus it was wakan to point a gun at any one in sport, to throw gunpowder into the fire, to whittle or hack a stick of fuel while one end was on fire, to threaten to kill a relative, though only in jest. Indeed, a thousand things that were considered dangerous or improper were wakan.

To say a thing was wakan was to give a sufficient reason why it should not be done, for these sayings had been repeated until they had become a part of the popular creed. These maxims could be learned only by familiar intercourse with the Indians, and they attracted the attention of white people much less than the ceremonies attending their religious feasts and dances; but they had far more influence over the everyday conduct of the people. Some of them were foolish notions, no more sensible than that to which allusion has been made, about beginning a work on Friday; but many of them were good rules for the regulation of the conduct, and things prohibited as wakan generally were such things as ought not to be done.

If any seemed disposed to disregard these warnings, the elders related to them the sad experience of those who had presumptuously trifled with things wakan. As a specimen of these illustrative anecdotes, one is here given.

One morning a young man asked his brother to go hunting with him, but the latter refused. When, after being urged to go, he still persisted in his refusal, he threatened to kill him if he did not go. The father, who overheard this, said, "Stop, my son, that is wakan." The son, however, made light of the admonition and said that, though the gods were ever so many, he did not believe they would hear him when he spoke so low. He went out without his brother, but when he returned at night, as he drew near home, in attempting to shoot a bird, he accidentally killed his brother.

It would seem that there were not only some who made light of the wakan prohibitions, which occasionally were indeed unworthy of regard, but there were also skeptics who did not have much confidence in some of their objects of worship, as we may infer from the following story, told for the encouragement of those who prayed to stones and in warning to those who despised them.

As two young men were going to war, they came to a stone and one of them prayed to it, saying, "Grant that I may kill an enemy and return safe." The other, who thought stones deaf and prayers addressed to them useless, said, "If you can do anything, have me killed." The prayers were both answered. One was killed, and the other returned triumphant.

These are abridged specimens of a store of anecdotes related by the Dakotas. Whether treasured up from past experience, or artfully manufactured for the occasion, they furnish satisfactory proof of the folly of those who despised the traditions of their ancestors or the admonitions of their prophets. They had the same kind of proof for the efficacy of their religious practices as some farmers have for the belief that their turnips should not be sown or their bushes cut at a certain time of the moon, or as the beekeeper has, that if he sells any of his bees there is danger of selling his good fortune with them. The same sort of proof supports many of the popular delusions of civilized people. It is hard arguing against a formidable array of well authenticated assertions.

It was a custom of the Dakotas to abstain from eating certain birds or animals. For instance, a man might abstain from eating bear's flesh, or some particular part of the bear, and so of any other animal. This abstinence might be voluntary or enjoined by a prophet, and it might be temporary or perpetual.

They frequently made vows to abstain from certain kinds of food, and it was probably this habit of self-denial which enabled them to keep their pledges so well when they promised to abstain from the use of intoxicating liquors. They also fasted occasionally for religious reasons, abstaining entirely from the use of food; but it was not so easy to ascertain how much this was practiced, for they made no ostentatious show of fasting and were not communicative concerning their private devotions.

I have been describing the superstitions of the Dakotas, the inventions of the wakan-men. These were dark enough, a maze of falsehoods in which there were no glimmerings of light or truth, and they were the only part of their religion which attracted the attention of superficial observers.

But Cicero says that philosophers always make a distinction between superstition and religion. As a people, the Dakotas held certain opinions concerning religious subjects which were rather vague and defective than erroneous. These views or convictions were the remains of a clearer light which they had once possessed, or were the natural suggestions of reason and conscience.

The great mass of the people evidently believed in a superintending, overruling Providence, by which the world is governed and men often rewarded according to their deeds. It was very common for them to predict that some great calamity would befall the notoriously wicked. They were also accustomed to point out examples where great sins had been followed by severe punishments. These retributions they did not ascribe to any of the gods whom they ordinarily worshipped in public.

Moral delinquencies were not supposed to be very offensive to these imaginary beings. Their displeasure was incurred rather by the transgression of arbitrary rules; for example, the smoking of the wrong pipe, or at the wrong time, might provoke them more than theft or murder. It was as dangerous for the Dakotas to omit any of the prescribed ceremonies in the wakan-feast as it is for some Christians to eat meat on Friday.

The punishment of the wicked was ascribed to Taku-wakan, that is, some supernatural or divine power, though Taku-wakan was not a proper name and had no personal signification. This Taku-wakan had such a meaning in the minds of the Indians that none of us hesitated to use it when speaking of the providence of

God. The Dakotas could not be said to have any clear idea of the attributes of the Deity, but they did believe in a superintending righteous Providence. Although this belief was vague and undefined, it was real and universal, and so strong as to exert great influence over their conduct.

Evil deeds which provoked this unknown power to anger were not always of the same class with those which were punished by the gods of the wakan-men, but were transgressions of the divine law, what we call sins; and they believed that by this power individuals, families, nations, were punished for their iniquities. They sometimes said that they had been restrained from carrying out some wicked purpose by the fear of Taku-wakan; and they told of many individuals and families who had been destroyed by this mysterious power because of their wickedness. It was believed that whole bands were sometimes destroyed for their misdeeds.

They say that long ago some chiefs and principal men of the Iowas returned from Canada to Prairie du Chien in the winter, and attempted to pass through the Dakota territory to their own country. They were kindly received and hospitably entertained by the Wabashaw band, who sent messengers to the Wahpekutas, then encamped at Dry Wood, requesting them to receive the Iowas in a friendly manner and to aid them in their journey. The Wahpetukas returned a favorable answer and prepared a feast for the Iowas, but killed them all while they were eating it. This band of Dakotas was afterward very unfortunate. Many of them have been killed by the Sacs, and in one way and another they have been almost all cut off. These extraordinary calamities which befell them were attributed by the Dakotas to their wickedness, and especially to their barbarous massacre of the Iowas. Probably I should never have heard of that murder if the Dakotas had not mentioned it as the cause of the evils which befell the descendants of the assassins more than a hundred years after the offense was committed.

The Dakotas were quick to discern between right and wrong, and knew very well what to approve and what to condemn. As a general rule, whatever is regarded as a vice or a crime among white Americans was viewed in the same light by them. They did not need to be taught that theft, lying, adultery, and murder are wrong, any more than we do. Their consciences were not very sensitive, but they were generally capable of forming a correct judgment of the moral character of actions. When any did them wrong they were loud in their complaint, and never excused the offender on the ground that he was ignorant of what was right.

The religion taught them by the wakan-men had no connection with morality and no tendency to make them better. Whatever correct ideas they had of religion or morality were not in consequence of their superstitions, but in spite of them. It was the protest of conscience and common sense against the teachings of lying fables.

BELIEF IN IMMORTALITY.

Though they said little about a future state of retribution, they had a firm belief in the immortality of the soul. Their views of the nature of the future state, and of the condition of departed spirits, were necessarily confused and uncertain; but they expected to exist hereafter, and to go to what they called "the country of spirits." It was to them an unknown country, but a real one. To go to the land of ghosts was a common phrase, signifying to die, and they spoke of the dead as "dwelling in the land of spirits." To say, "I shall go as a spirit," was the same as to say, "I shall die." The bright line of light among the stars which we call "the milky way" they call "the path of spirits."

Many of the religious doctrines propounded by us, as missionaries, they received with doubt and distrust, because new to them; but when we spoke of the existence of the soul after the death of the body, what we said awakened neither doubt nor surprise, for the immortality of the soul was with them an article of popular belief. Here we stood on common ground. I have heard two or three deny the belief of immortality, but this was done in a spirit of contradiction, for the doctrine was believed as universally by them as by us.

What some of them said about each person having several souls, was, I think, the contrivance of some inventive genius to explain difficulties and reconcile inconsistencies. If the soul had departed to the land of ghosts, and at the same time hovered about the grave, and also remained where the lock of hair was kept, it seemed necessary that there should be more than one spirit, to inhabit all these places at once. The doctrine of a plurality of souls explained or obviated this difficulty. Perhaps such a theory is needed by some of our own people, who believe that the spirit returns to God who gave it, lingers about the graveyard, and haunts also old houses and ruins, maliciously frightening benighted travelers. Plenty of irreconcilable and inexplicable notions about ghostly matters may be found afloat among any people, if they are sought for.

Whatever some individual Dakotas, when hard pressed by embarrassing questions, may have said about several souls belonging to one person, or to each individual, is not to be taken as the common faith of the people. It was evidently the popular belief that each individual had one soul, and not, as some have affirmed, that each one was to be divided into three or four distinct beings after death. From the common conversation of the people no one would ever learn or suspect that they believed a man has more than one soul. They speak of the soul of man just as we do, as one and identical with the body to which it belonged. Of the resurrection of the body they of course knew nothing.

A belief in transmigration of souls prevailed to some extent among the Dakotas, but seemed to amount to little more than a notion that some had existed as men or beasts before being born into this world. This idea is to be classed with the lying fables of their false prophets, rather than with the articles of popular belief.

To add to their importance, some of their wakan-men remembered having signalized themselves in some pre-existent state. The persons who had transmigrated from one state of existence to another, claimed in some instances that in their former state they were wild beasts; others affirmed that they were Indians, and others white men. Those who had been white persons, were too little acquainted with the character and customs of the whites to give a satisfactory account of their experiences as members of a civilized community. Their accounts may, however, have satisfied the Dakotas, if they are not more discriminating than their white neighbors; for it does not require a very intimate acquaintance with Indians to qualify one to write a description of them that will gain credence with the public.

Some were reminded that they had lived before by events occurring in this life. For instance, if one unexpectedly recovered after being severely wounded, he might remember having been a grizzly bear or some other animal that is not easily killed. In speaking of a past state of existence, they invariably used the word which signifies to dream, which might imply that the pre-existence was imaginary rather than real.

The Dakotas had that instinctive dread of death that is common to all, but they had only the most vague and confused notions about a future state of retribution. Some current sayings proved that they thought some crimes committed in this world might be punished in the life to come. They had a common saying that whatever one stole in this world, he would be compelled to carry in the next; and they would sometimes say of a notorious thief that his ghost would have a heavy load to carry in the future state. They seemed to think that the suicide, who hung herself, would have to wear around her neck, in the world of spirits, the cord by which she was strangled.

These and other like sayings proved that they had some expectation of retribution after death, but it was difficult to learn how much they feared future punishment. They were no more free to converse on such subjects than are white persons, who, conscious of their guilt, can think of a day of righteous judgment only with apprehension. It is not probable that many of them had any very alarming apprehensions of being called to account hereafter for the deeds done in the body; but their thoughts and feelings concerning such subjects they kept mostly to themselves, and their fears of a coming judgment might have been greater than they appeared to be.

The public is familiar with many written compositions which have been published from time to time, purporting to set forth the ideas entertained by Indians concerning the beauties and delights of the Spirit Land. These romances may contain beautiful sentiments and delightful descriptions of that happy world, but those who are well acquainted with Indians will hardly believe that the sentiments or descriptions originated with them. A foundation for the statements they contain may have been furnished by interpreters, who were often annoyed by questions to which they could give no satisfactory answers without inventing one themselves or repeating what they had read. When the half-breed interpreter was asked by an inquisitive visitor what the Indians thought about another world, he did not like to tell how little he knew about the matter; but he chose rather to conceal his own ignorance, and to gratify the inquirer at the same time, by giving such an answer as he knew would be more satisfactory than the true one. The writer speaks from experience, having been himself thus imposed upon.

Fables furnished by interpreters and others to gratify the curious and inquisitive, and to save their own credit, when exaggerated and embellished by ingenious and unscrupulous writers, become agreeable romances and give delightful descriptions of that heaven to which the Indian is supposed to look forward with longing anticipations. But the Indian, himself, knew of no such abode of the blessed. The Spirit Land was full of terrors for him, and his death song was not a song of triumph.

RECREATIONS.

Some things which have been already mentioned, under the head of religion and worship, might perhaps with equal propriety be classed with diversions. Indeed they are so combined that it is difficult to draw a line between them. We can hardly tell whether Christmas and Thanksgiving partake more of a secular or of a religious character, whether they are times set apart for recreation or devotion; and so it was with many of the observances of the Dakotas. Solemn religious ceremonies might serve to introduce joyous festivals or sportive pastimes.

The Dakotas carried their religion into almost everything, for, unlike the Christian religion, it was of such a nature that it was never out of place. There was no incongruity between it and the most thoughtless levity or reckless dissipation.

Yet they had some recreations with which religious ceremonies were not mingled, and the most conspicuous and popular of these was the ball-play. When this game was played, sometimes all the active and able-bodied men were engaged in it, the middle-aged making up in skill and dexterity what they lacked in agility. If only the men of one village played, they divided into two equal parties; but often one band or subdivision of the tribe challenged another, or two small bands entered the lists against one large one.

With slight changes, this Dakota game is much played in Canada, and occasionally in England and the United States, under the name of lacrosse. Pike mentioned it as played by the Dakotas in 1805 on a beautiful prairie which became the site of the city of

La Crosse, Wisconsin. This city took its name from the ball game, which itself is so called from the peculiar ball-club and net, named by the French "la crosse."

The ball-club was made of hickory, bent at one end into a small hoop, about three inches in diameter, across which several strings were tied, crossing each other in the center of the hoop, and forming a little net with which they picked up the ball and threw it. The length of the club was proportioned to the height of the owner, but did not vary much from three feet. The ball was non-elastic, often made of wood, and not so large as that commonly used by ballplayers. The net in which the ball was held was only an inch or two in depth, so that a slight blow on the club caused the ball to fall out of it.

A smooth level place was selected on the prairie, and two parallel boundaries were fixed nearly half a mile apart. The aim of one of the parties was to throw the ball over one of these boundaries; and of the other, to throw it over the opposite one. The players wore no clothing save a breech-cloth and moccasins, but were gaily painted. Many wore bunches of ribbons or feathers, fastened to their belts behind, which fluttered like streamers when they ran, but which were often scattered in fragments on the field before the game was over.

The ball was first carried to the center of the playground and tossed into the air, and to whatever place it fell there was a general rush, followed by a clattering of clubs, each trying to pick it up himself, or to frustrate the attempts of others to get it. None might touch the ball with the hands, and there was generally a long struggle over it before any one could succeed in throwing it, for if one caught it on his club, some one of the opposite party was likely to knock it out before he could give it a toss. When it was finally thrown by one more adroit or more lucky than the rest, wherever it fell there was another rush for it, and another struggle over it.

If the ball fell, as it sometimes did, where there were few or no players, the one who first reached it had an opportunity to throw it far toward his own line, and if possible toward one of his own party; or, if he was a fleet runner and the way clear, he ran with it as far as possible, sometimes quite to the limit of the playground. But the players of both parties were so scattered over the ground that it was seldom possible for the swiftest runner to carry the ball far, without having it knocked out of his club by some active opponent; and if he failed to throw it soon enough, he had no chance to throw it at all. Thus the ball was carried, or thrown, back and forth across the playground, now almost to the limit on one side, then intercepted and thrown b again, until finally it passed over one of the boundaries, when the players might take breath, for one point of the game was lost and won. After resting a few minutes, the ball was again tossed up. and the game was resumed.

It is not strange that the Dakotas should have been fascinated with their ball plays. No such interest can be felt in any of our ball games as was excited by these Indian games. It was an animating sight to see a hundred men or more, painted with various colors, with their gay streamers floating in the breeze, and displaying all their muscular powers to the best advantage. True they were nearly naked, but they were quite as well clothed as the competitors in the old Grecian games. This would have been one of the most celebrated games in the world if it had been played by the ancient Greeks and described by Homer.

A great crowd of spectators, often nearly all the inhabitants of two or three villages, hovered around the field, watching with deep anxiety the progress of the game, and were elated or depressed as the ball went this way or that across the playground. They had often more staked on the game than the players themselves had. It was a fair field for the display of all athletic qualities, of force, speed, skill and dexterity. Each actor was stimulated to do his best, because hundreds were watching to see who failed and who excelled, and each was anxious to save the property he had staked and to win that of his neighbor. Loud applause or sharp censure was heard from the surrounding multitudes, as they witnessed some skillful feat or awkward blunder; and the shouts of the eager contestants, as they surged back and forth or crowded together around the ball, were heard far away.

This favorite game was not only a test of the physical qualities of the actors, but was also a severe trial of their tempers. It was a rude game, and those engaged in such a strife could not be expected to deal gently with all around them. There was crowding, accidental blows from ball clubs were received, also collisions of men running at full speed, and many other unavoidable accidents, so that frequently, as the game progressed and the excitement increased, one after another might be seen to leave the scene of action with a halting gait and take his place among the spectators. When there were many engaged in the play, seldom, perhaps never, all escaped unhurt. Complaints were sometimes made of carelessness or harshness, but generally injuries were borne good-naturedly. The game might be soon decided by the defeat of one of the parties, but it was more likely to continue till all were glad to have it end and indeed needed several days of rest.

The women had their ball-plays too, but in a different style from that of the men. They knocked the ball with clubs upon the ice of a frozen lake or river. Many of them were skillful players, and some were swift runners; but their motions were impeded by their dress, and their playing did not attract as much attention as that of the men. They commonly bet heavily on their games, and were too anxious to win to preserve an equanimity of temper. As they were not all remarkable for self-control, their games sometimes ended in disputes.

In the summer, girls sometimes amused themselves by playing little games with such clubs as were used by the men.

I have been particular in describing the ball-play, because it was the only athletic sport in which the Dakotas seemed to feel much interest, excepting foot-races. Some of their foot-races were very long, being designed to test the endurance as well as the speed of the runners.

Young men and boys amused themselves by shooting at targets with bows and arrows. Wrestling and boxing they did not practice. They very rarely struck each other with their fists on any occasion, but, instead of boxing, they had a fashion of hitting with the feet. It was done by running near another, and hitting him with the bottom of the foot while passing by him. To hit an enemy in this manner was counted the same as to touch him with the hand. Only the boys practiced this as a diversion.

· The children had few games worth mentioning. The boys amused themselves in the summer with bows and arrows, which they always carried with them. If they found no game to shoot, they shot at marks.

In the winter they slid down hill. The boy made his sled of a piece of bark, or of a barrel stave, if he could get one. A hole was bored through the forward end, in which a string was tied, and the owner, holding the cord in his hand and standing erect on his narrow sled, with one foot before the other rode boldly down the steepest hills.

They had a way of fashioning sticks in such a shape that when thrown on the snow or ice, they glanced off and flew to a great distance. Both young men and boys were very fond of this diversion.

GAMBLING.

Betting on the ball game has been already mentioned. A very large amount of property, that is, a large amount for so poor a people, might be staked on a single game, especially when one band played against another. The stakes consisted of almost any kind of property in their possession, such as clothing, traps, guns, kettles, and horses. The property wagered was often literally staked, being hung on stakes within sight of the playground. If anyone had anything which he wished to stake, it was thus displayed for the inspection of the public. Then whoever wished to bet on the other side might bring some article and put with it. The one making the challenge could refuse to stake his property against a thing of less value. But this was frequently done.

The favorite game of chance with the men was commonly played with a bullet and mittens, though the name of the game indicates that moccasins were originally used instead of mittens, and it was doubtless played before bullets were known to the Dakotas. Four mittens were laid down in a row, and a bullet having been concealed in one of them by one of the parties, it was the business of the other party to tell which mitten contained the ball. Of course there was but one chance of four that the guesser would hit it right, but when one succeeded in finding the ball it was his turn to hide it. The gambling parties were often very large, but only one on each side was chosen to play. The others watched the turns of fortune and sang a tune that was appropriate to this game, which was always sung when it was played, accompanied by a drum. The

Dakotas often became very much absorbed in this gambling, and continued it many nights in succession.

Though it was a mere game of chance, they did not all so regard it, but thought the result might be affected by magical incantations. I was once with a hunting party which encamped several days with a band of Ojibways, and the men of both parties spent many nights in gambling. The Ojibways won considerable property from the Dakotas, causing much dissatisfaction, and the Dakota chief told me that he was afraid we should have serious trouble about it. The Dakotas did not accuse the Ojibways of cheating, but some of them said the games were won by witchcraft. The incantations used by the Ojibway player were very simple, for he merely dipped his fingers in ashes and blew upon and examined them before touching the mitten, which he did with a wise and mysterious look. However, as these maneuvers were followed by success, it was natural that the Dakotas should suppose that they had some efficacy.

Women did most of their gambling with plum-stones, which had certain marks burnt upon them. The plum-stones were a kind of dice, and after they had been shaken up in a wooden dish, the latter was set down suddenly so that the jar caused them to rebound. This was also a game of pure chance, but the players seemed to think that hissing sounds and waving the hands over the dish might in some way influence the result.

The young men learned to play cards, but did not gamble with them much at the time referred to.

The evils of gambling were in some respects the same as with other people. They wasted their time, and sometimes lost what they could not well spare; but they had no large fortunes to lose, and children were not robbed of their inheritance by the reckless ventures of their fathers. The loss of property which they incurred was not irreparable, and caused only temporary inconvenience. There were no professional gamblers among them, and probably no cheating; but their games were such that, excepting the ball-play, chance alone determined the result.

Nearly all the men in a village would occasionally be devoted for a season to gambling, and then all at once they would leave it and turn their attention to something else. The women, when at leisure, spent much time over their plum-stones; and in warm weather some would sit in the shade, rattling these dice for a half a day at a time. When one was bankrupt or tired of playing, another would take her place. Unlike the men, they had no music at their games; and not many, generally only two, were interested in the result of the game. They were very still and quiet in their gambling, seldom disputing, bearing their losses better than one would expect. The maiden handed over some favorite ornament to the winner with a little sadness in her countenance, and perhaps with a half suppressed sigh, but bore her loss in silence. They staked small articles, such as beads, earrings, and other ornaments, and occasionally things of better value. Like the men, they had their fits of periodical gambling, and a greater portion of the time it was laid aside and not permitted to interfere with their usual avocations.

Social Feasts.

Such feasts as were attended by many religious ceremonies have been already described, and there remains to be described only the social feast, or the "calling together," as the Indians named it. This important feast was attended with few formalities, and was conducted in a rational and agreeable manner. It was held in one of the largest tents or houses, and as many were invited as could be accommodated. If the village or camp was not very large, all the men might be called together. When the food was prepared, a herald stepped out into the middle of the village or camp, and, after gaining attention by singing the proper tune, he called, in a loud voice, each guest by name. After repeating the name he said, "I call you to the feast." I never saw women at these feasts. The food was often roasted venison, but any other food might be used. It was divided as equally as convenient among the persons present, and the allotments were large or small, according to the amount of food in proportion to the number invited, for it was not considered necessary to provide a full meal. Custom allowed each guest to eat his portion at the feast, or to carry it home, as he might prefer. Consultations were held at these feasts, and matters of common interest were discussed and decided.

It was in these assemblies that the chief frequently ascertained what course would be acceptable to a majority of his band, and he issued his orders or made his proclamations accordingly. These were the proper places for consultation, the popular councils. When they met to consider matters of great public interest, it was considered necessary to have as many of the men present as possible; but if the matter was of little importance, they were not so careful to have a full assembly.

The persons present at these councils did not always agree in their views of public matters, and there were sometimes animated discussions, but rarely noisy disputes. Young men seldom took an active part in the debates, but their responses or silence at the close of the speeches showed what their sentiments were. Those who were overruled acquiesced in the decisions of the majority, or yielded to the wishes of the more persistent or influential, though not always without a little private grumbling. The disagreement in council might be so great that it was necessary to adjourn without coming to a decision. If both parties obstinately adhered to their own opinions concerning the matter in dispute, the same measure might be debated in several successive councils.

The character of the Dakotas was exhibited in a very different light in these meetings from that which marked their religious assemblies. The good sense, dignity, and decorum of the one appeared in strange contrast with the ridiculous absurdities of the other; but shrewdness in worldly matters and preposterous notions concerning things unseen are often found in the same person the world over.

THE WAR DANCE.

Some of their dances have been described in connection with worship, and most dances had religious ceremonies connected with them.

Performers in the war dance painted their faces in such a manner as to render their appearance most frightful, and each one held some weapon in his hand. They stood with their knees bent, and kept time to the drum and rattle by short, quick jumps, lifting both feet from the ground at the same time. When they stopped to breathe, some one would recount, in a loud voice and with appropriate gestures, his exploits in war. At intervals, the loud, abrupt, sharp notes of the war-whoop were heard. These dances were very violent exercise, and could not be continued long at a time. There was some variety in them, but they closely resembled each other.

Their main object in war dances seemed to be to render themselves as hideous and terrible as possible. In this they succeeded so well that persons of weak nerves, who were not acquainted with them, did not care to go very near them while the dance continued, even to gratify their curiosity to see how Indians look. Indeed no one, while viewing a war dance, would think it desirable to have them lay violent hands on him.

No easy or graceful movements were made in any of the Dakota dances. The motions of the men were unnatural, abrupt and violent, and the strength of the dancers was taxed to the utmost. None of their favorite recreations had any attractions for the indolent, effeminate, or feeble; but they were designed to afford the actors an opportunity to exhibit agility, strength, hardihood, and powers of endurance, qualities that were highly prized by the Dakotas.

SCALP DANCE.

This was one of the few dances in which both men and women participated, and in this they danced separately. Most of the dancing was done by the women, while the men stood by, singing the scalp tune and beating the drum. Usually some old women seized the staff to which the scalp was attached and led off the dance, and then the other females formed a circle and danced around her. The dancing performed by the females was characterized by gravity and decorum, with no such demonstrations of triumph and exultation as we might expect to see on such occasions. Their singing, however, had in it a sound of triumph. The female dancers, clothed in their best apparel, stood close together in a circle, with their blankets wrapped around them and their faces toward the center of the circle. They stood very straight, with serious countenances, having their eyes fixed on the ground before them.

In dancing they raised both feet simultaneously from the ground and jumped a few inches sideways. This was done by the action of the muscles of the ankles and feet alone, and in this way, standing perfectly straight and in close order and moving by each leap a few inches to the right, they kept time to the music and passed slowly around the circle. At certain stages of the dance, the men and women formed in two separate lines, facing each other, and danced back and forth, the two lines alternately approaching each other and then again receding.

During all the time that the dance continued, the tune of the scalp dance was sung. The few words of the song were frequently repeated, and the women at intervals responded with short, shrill notes, which could be heard at a great distance. The character of the music was in keeping with the nature of the dance. When heard in the darkness, the ceaseless reverberations of the drum, the loud defiant notes of the men, and the shrieking chorus of the women, as they rose on the night air, made such music as we might expect from those who could dance with delight around the scalps of the dead.

The dancing of the men was in a very different style from that of the women. It was never very agreeable, and was sometimes disgusting to the beholder. To the civilized eye, the whole performance had a fiendish aspect, and, unlike most of their dances, was often continued far into the night. This furnished a convenient opportunity for illicit intercourse between the sexes; for, in the excitement and confusion of the dance, some of the dancers might slip off into the darkness without being missed. The more thoughtful of the Indians complained of the demoralizing influence of the scalp dance when held in the night. Are any of our dances similarly demoralizing?

SMOKING.

It is well known to the public, not only that Indians are inveterate smokers, but that the pipe is made to occupy a prominent place in the transaction of important business. They often expended great labor in making and ornamenting pipes and pipe-stems, especially such as were to be used on great occasions or to be presented to important personages. So much is known about this public use of the pipe, that I shall only describe their manner of smoking. They smoked the dried bark of dogwood, mixed with a small proportion of tobacco. They had smoked from time immemorial, and, when first discovered by white men, raised their own tobacco. They inhale the smoke, drawing it into the lungs, and often breathing it out through the nostrils.

Tobacco alone is too strong to be used in this way, and the common clay pipe is too short, as the smoke from it is too warm for the lungs. A very few whiffs drawn into the lungs suffice for the time, and a single small pipeful answers for several persons. Their pipes are made of the red pipestone; and the stems, which were two or three feet long, were made of young ash trees, the pith being bored out with a wire. Most Dakotas carried their pipes when travelling or hunting, but at such times did not smoke very often.

Few of the young women smoked, and boys did not generally smoke until grown up. The Dakotas used much less tobacco than white men who smoke, but did not like to be long without their pipes, and when a company were together pipes were passed around frequently. The bowls of the pipes were not very large, but a single pipeful served for ten or fifteen to smoke, though in a company of men, especially of old men, the pipe was passed around at very short intervals. Their pipes were commonly ignited by lighting a small piece of touch-wood with the flint and steel; and they were so accustomed to this that I have seen them light their pipes in this manner while sitting by the fire.

WARS.

The war parties of the Dakotas were composed of volunteers following volunteer leaders. When one wished to lead out a war party, he gave notice that he had been directed to do so by some god from whom he had received information of the manner in which the affair should be conducted, and of the results of the expedition. This information was communicated by him in guarded, ambiguous language, metaphorical figures being used, so that the interpretation could be made to correspond with future events. Some of the revelations were contrived with as much subtlety as the answers of the ancient oracles. The leader also continued to receive, from time to time, such revelations as were needed on the march.

If the event did not correspond with the prediction, the prophet could save his reputation by attributing the failure to the misconduct of some of his followers, by which his tutelary god was offended; and, if there happened to be an agreement between the prophecy and the event, his reputation as a true prophet was established. It required a shrewd man to so manage as not to run the risk of being considered an impostor, and some of these pretended prophets lost all credit with the people; but others contrived, even when unsuccessful, to return with a good reputation.

Probably not all the followers of these leaders believed in their inspiration, but they were willing that the timid and inexperienced should be animated with the confidence and hopes which such belief afforded. After all they used their own judgment, managing their expeditions very much as though the gods had nothing to do with them. We can hardly believe that such generals as Pompey and Caesar were much governed in their movements by the reports of the augurs who accompanied the Roman armies. It was little to them what signs were found in the entrails or vitals of the victims that were slain, but many of the common soldiers were doubtless very much inspired by a favorable report from the augurs. It was useless for a man of inferior abilities to pretend that he had been chosen to lead a war party, for they confided more in the natural abilities of the man than in the supernatural wisdom imparted to him by the gods. They would not follow a fool, though he claimed to be led by all the gods known to their mythology.

As these war parties were composed of volunteers, they might be large or small, according to circumstancs. Sometimes, though very rarely, quite an army might be collected, composed of most of the men from several villages; but it was not common for many to go together to war. Most of the men might have something else to attend to, might be apprehensive of an attack from the enemy, or think the expedition ill-timed or unadvisable.

It was not thought good policy to send out large war parties, for it was difficult to keep them supplied with provisions, and they were in danger of being discovered too soon by the enemy. Young men who had never killed an enemy were most anxious to go to war, though they were made to act as servants for the veteran warriors. Women sometimes accompanied the men, but very seldom. They did not go to fight but to mangle the bodies of the slain, and none went except those who had lately had friends killed by the enemy and panted for revenge, or some old hag who resembled a woman only in form.

Guns and knives were chiefly depended upon in fighting, but hatchets and war-clubs and especially the consecrated spear were carried by war parties and all were more or less used. Spears were doubtless much used by their ancestors and had a traditionary importance, but could not have been so much depended upon after the introduction of fire-arms.

Shields made of raw hides had been used formerly, but were laid aside when the arrow was superseded by the bullet. Arrows were not entirely discarded, however, as they could be discharged more rapidly than guns or rifles and made no noise.

They carried some provisions, and while they were far from the haunts of the enemy killed what game they could conveniently; but when they passed out of their own territory all hunting ceased and no fires were kindled. Strict rules were adopted and were rigidly enforced, and, if necessary, severe measures were used to secure subordination and keep all in their places. If they wished to cross rivers that were not fordable, they made little rafts large enough to carry their arms and baggage, and, swimming behind them, pushed them across the stream.

Fleet and reliable scouts, sent out by two and two, were kept always in advance of the main party, and returned from time to time to report. These scouts had a difficult and dangerous service to perform. They were to see without being seen, for, while it was important that they should discover the enemy, it was equally important that the enemy, as watchful and wary as they, should not discover them. While hunting for others, they might themselves be waylaid and shot. If only their tracks were seen, it might render the whole expedition abortive. They were not hunting white men, but Indians, who join all the intelligence and cunning of a man with all the alertness of a wild beast that is hunted, and sometimes scouts that were sent out never came back.

When any of the enemy were discovered, the utmost pains were taken to approach them unperceived. This was no easy matter, for they were more watchful than deer, and a surprise was made more difficult by the fact that where a scalp was to be taken each one wanted a chance to take it and was unwilling to remain behind while others secured the trophies.

If the enemy discovered was away from home, as hunters out hunting, they killed them as soon as possible, and taking the scalp or scalps, started for home in haste. By that time they were likely to be out of provisions and too much fatigued to feel any disposition to tarry long enough to give the enemy time to rally and pursue them. If, however, the party was a strong one, most of them might lie in ambush, while a few showed themselves and tried to draw the enemy into the snare and kill more. This stratagem was not often successful, for they had enemies to deal with who knew all the wiles of savage warfare.

On discovering a camp of the enemy, they were careful to ascertain their number and probable strength. If they thought them too strong for an open attack, they lay in wait, hoping to catch one or more of them away from the camp, and to get off without being overtaken. In this they often succeeded, and most of their scalps were taken in this way. It was not always necessary for them to lie in ambush near the camp, but they took their station near some well-beaten path, perhaps several miles from the tents, so that if they killed an enemy they might get a good start for home before avengers started in pursuit.

They might be prevented from attacking a camp by the difficulty of approaching it, for the Indians located their summer villages in the most secure places, often on islands. In such cases nothing could be done more than to cut off some luckless straggler, unless the main body could be enticed into an ambush; but Indians are not easily drawn into an ambush, and their excessive fear of being waylaid often prevented their pursuing an enemy when they might have done so with success.

When they dared not make an open attack and despaired of falling in with any stragglers, they fired into the tents in the night and fled under cover of the darkness. This was done once at Kaposia by Hole-in-the-Day, but firing into tents and running away was not considered a very brave exploit, and they who did it gained little honor and no trophies.

After examining the enemies' camp, if they found no obstacle in the way of an attack and concluded that they were able to overcome them, they waited until daybreak. All the reconnoitering was done by one or two, while the rest of the party lay concealed, often several miles away. They did not attack in broad daylight, because they could not then make their approach unseen, and their enemies would be better prepared to fight or flee; nor did they make an assault in the night, lest in the confusion of the fight they should injure each other, and lest many of their enemies should escape in the darkness. They made it an invariable rule, when practicable, to begin an assault at early dawn, for, though they would be likely to find a larger number asleep at an earlier hour, they could then better distinguish their friends from their foes, and could see those who attempted to escape.

In preparing for an assault, they threw off most of their clothes and painted their bodies so that they could recognize each other in the tumult and confusion of the fight. The paint and war-whoop served instead of uniforms, enabling them to discriminate during the battle between friends and enemies, for each tribe had a war-cry of its own. In commencing the attack at break of day, the assailants had greatly the advantage, as their enemies could be shot down before they could prepare to defend themselves, and if any attempted to escape they could be seen and killed. But Indians were so quick to seize their arms, and fought with such desperation when there was no hope of escape, that the attacking party could hardly expect to kill many of them without losing some of their own number. Indians were not slaughtered like sheep without any attempt at resistance, as many of the white settlers on our frontier were in 1862.

To be awakened suddenly out of sleep by the report of fire-arms, the yells of the assailants, and the whizzing of bullets, mingled with groans of the dying and shrieks of women and children, was well calculated to fill the mind with consternation; but the Indian was generally true to himself in such emergencies, and, though the women might be wild with terror, the men thought only of fighting. When there was no hope of escape and nothing else to fight for, they fought for vengeance.

Even after a man was shot down and mortally wounded, it was dangerous to go near him so long as he could wield a knife, for he might kill another while he was dying himself. An old man at Lac qui Parle told me that he knew a Dakota killed by a very old Ojibway, who had no weapon but a knife with a broken blade not an inch in length. An Ojibway camp had been taken by assault, and the old man was found sitting in one of the tents. The Dakota, supposing him to be so old and descrepit as to be unable to make any defence, carelessly laid hold of him to kill him, when the old man seized his antagonist and drew the broken knife across his abdomen, giving him a mortal wound.

The Dakotas felt little compassion for their enemies, and doubtless sometimes tortured them. A chief once told me that when a young man he helped throw Ojibway children into the flames of their burning houses. That must have been about the year 1790, and it is the only case of torture I recollect to have heard of among them; but if they tortured one they might another, and they were cruel enough to do it. No one acquainted with them would have been surprised to learn that they were in the habit of tormenting their prisoners of war, for there were among them men as vindictive and cruel "as e'er clenched fingers in a captive's hair." We have, however, no proof that any such practice was common among them. Certainly it was not so common here as among the tribes farther east, unless those Indians have been greatly calumniated.

The Jesuit missionaries, writing of the Dakotas more than two hundred years ago, say, "The Dakotas are more generous than the Algonquins and Hurons, and, seeming satisfied with the glory of victory, restore the captives they have taken without reward." They very rarely, if ever, tried to prolong the agonies of those whom they killed, but despatched them at once, and cut their dead bodies in pieces. Their traditionary rules required that when an assault was made it should be a surprise, sudden, bold, and decisive. The combatants could not win the highest honor by standing at a distance and shooting at the enemy. It was not he who shot a man, but he who first touched him, to whom they accorded the chief credit of killing him. The rules by which military honors were awarded to the successful warriors were evidently designed to make all press forward and strive to be foremost.

It was considered most honorable to be the first to touch an enemy, but the three next following were accounted as having helped kill him, though he might be dead before they reached him. These four who first touched the enemy wore eagle feathers in token of their prowess.

While those who were in front pressed eagerly forward, they were sure of being well supported by others who were as anxious as they to win laurels. If the credit of killing had been given only to the foremost, others, seeing him in advance, would not have had the same motive for supporting him, and might have hesitated about exposing themselves to danger when no honor was to be gained.

One who shot a man but did not touch him, wore a feather, but with a mark to denote that the wearer had not come in actual contact with him. Some of these rules of warfare were probably very ancient, having been adopted when they used no weapons but those of their own manufacture, and when it was more difficult to kill men without coming to close quarters than it is with fire-arms. This may account for those regulations which were designed to bring the warriors as quickly as possible into close contact with the enemy.

The Dakotas, when first heard of by white men, had an established reputation for skill and bravery in battle, and that reputation was probably well earned. Though they were extremely cautious before and after a battle, their military rules required that when an assault was actually made, the assailants should throw their whole force on the enemy at once and make short work of it.

Doubtless in former times many a camp of their hostile neighbors was swept by them in an instant as with the besom of destruction, but in modern times their mode of fighting must have been considerably modified to adapt it to the use of fire-arms. It was considered unmanly to shoot women and children, unless they were likely to escape by flight; and, unless they chose to take them captives, they commonly killed them with knives, spears, war-clubs, or hatchets. To seize a man who was not wounded and kill him with a knife, was considered an act of bravery worthy of the highest applause, and the Dakotas sometimes needlessly lost their lives in attempting to kill wounded men with knives or clubs.

Red Bird, a noted warrior of the Lake Calhoun band, was killed in the battle, or rather slaughter, on Rum River by an Ojibway who had been shot down and was lying on the ground. Knowing that he was alive, Red Bird was anxious to be the first to reach him, and, though warned of the danger by others who knew that the Ojibway's gun was loaded, he rushed on and was killed.

When a war party unexpectedly found itself in the presence of a strong force of the enemy and an attack was apprehended, intrenchments were made by digging pits in the ground, the earth being loosened up with knives and thrown out with the hands. They did not dig a long trench, but separate holes, each one selecting the place that best suited him. If they had time to finish their pits they dug them three or four feet deep, and if they found easy digging they did not require very much time and it was marvelous to see how rapidly they would throw out the earth.

The inhabitants of villages prepared in a similar way for defence against an apprehended attack from a war party, although when women and children were to be protected the pits were made large enough to accommodate families, the non-combatants sitting securely in the bottom of the trenches while the bullets whistled over their heads. I once passed a large camp of Indians in the evening and saw them dwelling quietly in their tents, but on visiting them again the next morning I found them all hidden in the ground. They had been alarmed in the night, and before daylight they were where hostile bullets could not reach them.

It will be understood, from what has been said in another place, that the number of eagle feathers worn by the Dakotas was about four times as great as the number of the enemy killed. There were seldom less than four in a war party, and, if the one who shot the enemy was not one of the four who first touched him, there would be five feathers for one dead enemy. A man might be entitled to wear a great many feathers, even though he had never actually killed an enemy himself, so that the number of feathers on a warrior's head did not often exactly represent the number of foes whom he had slain.

In the confusion and excitement of battle, it sometimes happened that it was difficult to tell who shot a man, or who were the first four to touch him, for two might reach the spot so nearly at the same time that it was difficult to tell who was first. This uncertainty gave rise to some disputes, but they were generally amicably settled in councils, after all the evidence had been carefully examined. It was considered a greater exploit to kill a man than to kill a woman or a child, and a difference in the feathers worn indicated the different degrees of honor.

The feathers were taken from the tail of the eagle, and no one not entitled to them was permitted to wear them, or indeed would wear them, more than a private soldier would assume the uniform and insignia of rank of a major general. They were carefully preserved in cedar boxes, and were worn only on special occasions.

The scalps of the slain were always taken if possible, for if these trophies were not secured no honors were awarded. Nothing but the scalp was received as proof that an enemy had been killed, for if any other evidence had been admitted there would have been danger of imposition or exaggeration, when the war party was very small. When they were hard pressed by the enemy and had no time to take the whole scalp, they might seize a lock of hair and cut off a piece of skin with it. I have seen them dancing around such pieces, but they took the scalp entire if possible.

The Indian custom of bringing home the scalps of their enemies is certainly a barbarous one, and it is not strange that many severe things have been said about it; but the scalps were taken simply as proof that enemies had been killed, just as David brought the foreskins of the Philistines to Saul, or as a man who claims the bounty for killing a wolf shows its head as evidence that the wolf is dead. The warrior was stimulated to kill his tribe's enemies by the promise of a bounty, to be paid in badges of honor, and he could not claim the bounty till he had shown the scalp of the enemy as proof that he had killed him.

It is well that civilized soldiers are not required to exhibit such proofs of the deaths of their enemies, for it is only a barbarous practice; but we might be discouraged if we knew thus how little damage is actually done to our enemies, when yet we are assured by a report of our generals that they are almost annihilated.

In scalping a female, the Dakotas took only that part of the skin of the head on which the hair grows; but, from a man they took the skin of the whole head, except the nose and upper lip, the skin of the cheeks and chin being taken with the ears also attached to the scalp. It took some time to scalp a man properly; and, if they dared not stay where one was killed long enough to do it, they cut off the head and carried it with them till they had leisure to take off the scalp.

The scalps were tanned and the flesh side painted, and, hoops of suitable size being prepared, they were stretched by passing cords through holes near the edge of the skin and around the hoops. The hair was carefully combed, and a comb was tied to the hoop to be used when necessary. The hoop had a handle by which it was carried. The scalps, which were treated with a sort of superstitious reverence, no females except young girls and old women being allowed to touch them, were carried from village to village, that as many as possible might have an opportunity to dance around them, and were finally buried with great formality. The Dakotas complained that the Ojibways did not treat scalps with proper respect.

When, in an attack on the enemy, the Dakotas lost any of their number, they made no attempt to bring the dead bodies away or to conceal them; but their rules required them to bring off their wounded, and I never heard of a wounded man being left behind by a war party. How much soever they might be exhausted by marching and fighting, or however great the distance from home, they did not desert their wounded comrades, but made it a point of honor to bring them as far as possible, even when they knew that they were mortally wounded and would die on the way. When compelled to retreat under fire from the enemy, they laid the wounded on blankets, and four men ran with them, each taking hold of a corner of the blanket. If there were not enough bearers or for some other reason they could not carry them in blankets, they carried them by turns on their backs. When they were not hard pressed by the enemy, they made litters by taking two poles and tying sticks across them, covering the framework with blankets. These were carried by two men who walked between the poles, bearing them by straps passing over their heads or shoulders. If the retreat was in an open prairie country, four men carried the litter. As the war parties were generally small, it was a hard task to bring home the wounded.

If a wounded man died on the way home, they left his body where he died. In such cases they did not conceal the body, but dressed it as well as they could, painted the face, and placed the dead man in a sitting posture with his back against a tree, if there were any near, and his face toward the enemy. They were accustomed to say that the scalp belonged to the enemy and they would not defraud them of it, but probably that was not the original reason for adopting such a custom. If a Dakota was killed near home, the enemy was not permitted to take his scalp if his people could prevent it, and the body was brought home and buried; but it would have been bad policy to require war parties to bring home or bury their dead. They were commonly sufficiently exhausted without any useless expenditure of strength. The bones of those who were left were sometimes brought home by their friends and buried, but not often.

On the return of warriors from a successful expedition, they blackened their faces as though mourning for the death of a relative, and each one wore for a time a bunch of swan's down on his head. For a considerable time they were not permitted to accompany another expedition against the enemy.

In speaking of Dakota poetry, I gave the words of one scalp song, and will here insert another of these strange productions: "My dog was hungry, and I brought him a fat enemy." To explain the meaning of the words, I will state that a war party of Ojibways, after having killed a Dakota near the lower end of Lake Pepin, were pursued and four of their number killed, one of whom was brought to the trading post of Louis Rock and was eaten by his hogs.

After a scalp was brought home, as soon as words suitable to the occasion could be prepared, those who accompanied the expedition went from house to house and from village to village, singing. The song was short, but they sang chiefly by note and could sing as well without words as with them. The young warriors of the victorious party, especially such of them as had never been to war before, walked about very proudly, and were everywhere made welcome and feasted, and were treated with the greatest consideration.

No one without witnessing it, can realize what intense excitement was produced in a village by the return of a successful war party. The women manifested mingled feelings of exultation and terror, for they were never more apprehensive of a hostile visit from their enemies than immediately after some of them had been slain, and the sight of the scalps of others reminded them that their own might soon be taken. For a time every thing else was forgotten. The old men wanted to know every minute circum-

stance of the surprise or the fight, and especially how each one
was killed.

They would have been delighted with Homer's description of a
battle, for they were very inquisitive to know just how each wound
was given, and how each victim died. The warriors were required
to give a detailed account of their adventures and exploits, and
they generally made it a point of honor to tell the exact truth
without concealment or exaggeration.

If they had been against the Ojibways, we commonly soon
heard the Ojibway version of the affair, which seldom differed ma-
terially from the account given by the Dakotas. Sometimes they
had mortally wounded more than they knew of. The Dakotas
often spoke with contempt of the Ojibways, but were careful not
то presume too much upon their imbecility or cowardice. They acknowledged that there were brave men among them, and, when
any of them performed a daring feat, gave them credit for it.
They admired a brave man, whether he was a friend or foe. The
Sacs they held in high esteem for their valor.

War expeditions were seldom undertaken in the winter, because fire was then neces sary and they were in danger of being be-
trayed by the smoke. The old men, however, told of a strong party
which once in their youth went out in the winter and destroyed
several Ojibway camps in succession.

The warriors occasionally met together to recount their achieve-
ments. A post or tree was prepared on which each in turn recorded his exploits. Whatever he wished to relate, he portrayed as
well as he could in picture writing, and then gave a verbal ex-
planation accompanied by appropriate gestures. The pictures,
words, and gestures, altogether gave a vivid and impressive description of events, and served to keep in memory transactions
which might otherwise have been partially forgotten.

Although the Indians were so eager in the prosecution of war,
it was very seldom that many were killed, and a great slaughter
was a very remarkable event. The different tribes were well
matched against each other, and all were too cautious to be easily
surprised. During ten years, beginning with 1835, the Dakotas
had about eighty killed by their enemies, and they killed about
one hundred and fifty of the Ojibways, Sacs, and Pottawattamies.

Seventy of the Ojibways were slain at the massacre on Rum river, July 4, 1839, an event that could hardly have happened in the ordinary course of warfare.

Much has been said about the barbarous manner in which the Dakotas and their neighbors carried on their wars; but leaving out of the account the torture of prisoners, which certainly was not much practiced by the Dakotas, their mode was the only one by which war in their circumstances could be prosecuted. They had no prisons where captives could be confined, and it would have been about as safe to capture a man as to take a mad wolf into custody. He would soon have gone back to his own people carrying a scalp or two with him. If they brought home half-grown boys or adult women, such captives were very likely to escape and carry back important information to the enemy. If infants had been spared, they would have perished on the way home; and if small children were captured, they must be carried one or two hundred miles, through the wilderness, by men who were too much worn out by marching and watching to assume any unnecessary burden. There was no way in which the power of an enemy could be weakened except by killing or capturing them, and there were very few whom it was safe or expedient to capture. No fortresses, nor trains of luggage, nor parks of artillery, were to be seized.

It made little difference to them whether they drove the enemy or were driven by him, and they did not care who held the field of battle, if they only held the scalps. If they lost more than they killed, it was a defeat; but if they killed more than they lost, it was a victory, though the enemy should chase them a hundred miles. The empty honor of holding a battle-field was nothing to them.

They were so cautious in the prosecution of their wars that they have incurred the imputation of cowardice, but they used no needless caution. It would have been folly for them to undertake to carry on their wars after the fashion of civilized nations, for their circumstances were altogether different. Civilized armies do not always succeed well when they march against Indians, and the Dakotas could not have afforded to run the risk of such a defeat as Braddock's. It would have ruined them. A loss of eight or ten men from a little band must be severely felt by all in the village, for their families were left without property, to be supported by others who could hardly maintain their own. They were not only missed as hunters but as warriors, being needed both to support and to defend their families. When the warriors had an opportunity to strike an effective blow without great danger to themselves, they were expected to do it, but all rashness was discouraged and all doubtful conflicts avoided. Recklessness, as well as cowardice, was considered a base quality in a warrior.

The conduct of Indian warriors sometimes seems strange to us, because we forget the necessity they were under of being careful of their lives. Civilized nations may lose large armies and hardly miss them, but every Indian man was a soldier, and to lose the army was to lose every man capable of bearing arms. They would let an enemy escape when they knew they could kill him, because they were afraid of being drawn into an ambush, or because they could not afford to give two for one.

In the summer of 1839, two Ojibways waylaid and killed a Dakota near Lake Harriet, and, taking his scalp and two guns that he was carrying, concealed themselves near by in a thick cluster of young trees. The writer was on the ground soon after the man was killed, and in the course of half an hour about fifty armed Dakotas were gathered around the dead body. The tracks were plainly to be seen in the tall grass and led directly into the thicket, but the Ojibways were well armed, having each two guns, and the Dakotas did not molest them. They knew they could kill them but feared it would require the loss of a greater number of their own men, and started off fifty miles another way in quest of vengeance.

They were rather cautious than cowardly, and fought with desperation when they thought the occasion demanded it. The Ojibways would no doubt have been pleased to have the Dakotas adopt our military tactics and maxims. Nothing would have suited them better than to have them march into the forests and swamps of the upper Mississippi, in good military order, especially if led by such generals as Braddock or St. Clair.

With regard to the barbarities practiced by the Dakotas, they had no reason to believe that the white people generally disapproved of them. In their official character, the commanders of the garrison at Fort Snelling advised them to live in peace with their neighbors; but in their private intercourse with military men and others, the Dakotas learned that he who had performed the greatest exploits in war was most highly esteemed by them. The Dakotas might be told that it was wrong to kill women and children, but he who had the most eagle feathers on his head was sure to attract the most attention and also to be treated with the greatest consideration.

MARRIAGE CUSTOMS.

There were few formalities attending marriage, except the contract for the purchase of the bride. Wives were purchased, and it was as disreputable for a young woman to become the wife of one who had not purchased her, as it is with us for a woman to cohabit with a man without the ceremony of marriage. It was not, however, considered so disgraceful for a widow or a divorced woman to marry without being purchased. Women did not consider it disgraceful to be bought and sold. The higher the price paid for them, the better they were pleased, for the payment of a great price proved that they were esteemed valuable.

It is probable that the wishes of the young women were generally consulted, and that a due regard was paid to their preferences in making arrangements for their marriage, but not always. They were sometimes compelled to marry men whom they disliked, but probably no means of compulsion were used that are not sometimes employed for the same purpose among civilized people. Parents were not in the habit of dealing harshly with their children, and it was not safe to drive a spirited girl to extremities, as she might elope with one who was able to protect her; or, if there were no other way to escape, the gate of death stood always open and she might commit suicide. Though this was seldom done, it happened often enough to serve as a salutary warning to those who had young women to dispose of in marriage.

Doubtless there was commonly a mutual understanding and agreement between the parties to be married, but not always; and women were not unwilling to marry men with whom they were little acquainted, provided they liked their appearance and knew that they had a good reputation. Girls did not by any means admit that they had nothing to do in selecting their partners for life, and parents sometimes complained that their daughters were too fastidious in the choice of husbands.

Brothers claimed the right to dispose of their sisters in marriage, but where there were no brothers or none of a suitable age, parents or other relatives made the marriage contract. None paid so much for their wives as Jacob did for Rachel, but the young women generally brought higher prices than young men were able to pay without the aid of their friends. As among white men, so among the Dakotas, a lover might fail to obtain the object of his choice because he was not so rich as some of his neighbors. There was also another resemblance between the civilized and the savage, that a man might, after performing some warlike exploit, obtain for almost nothing the girl who had been refused when he offered a good price for her, military renown being accepted in lieu of other qualifications.

Almost any kind of property might be given in exchange for a wife, such as horses, guns, cloth, kettles, etc. When a man wished to purchase a wife, if he had not property enough of his own, he solicited contributions from his friends, and, gathering all together, carried and deposited them by the house where the woman whom he wished to purchase resided. If they were accepted, the bargain was soon completed, and the marriage consummated without further ceremony. If they were rejected, they were taken back and restored to the original owners. But if the woman and her friends could not agree either to accept or refuse the offer, the goods were left sometimes for several days awaiting a decision, until notice was given that the offer was accepted or rejected. In arriving at a decision, more regard was generally had to the character of the man than to the value of his presents.

The bridegroom, if a young man, took up his abode at the residence of the bride, and whatever game he killed was carried there. The reputation of a skillful and industrious hunter was, as it ought to be, a great help to him in obtaining a wife.

After marriage, a man was not permitted to look his wife's father or mother in the face, speak their names, or address his conversation directly to either of them. If it was necessary for him to speak of or to either of them, he used the plural instead of the singular number, and, in speaking to them, used the third instead of the second person. The same rule was observed by the parents in addressing or speaking of their sons-in-law or daughters-in-law, and by the woman toward the parents of her husband. This whimsical prohibition, so far as speaking the name was concerned, extended to a large circle of relatives, so that often when one asked the name of another, he was prevented from telling it by this absurd custom.

It is difficult to imagine any reason they could have for the adoption of such a rule, but this custom was not peculiar to the Dakotas. Intermarriages were not allowed within the circle of relatives embraced by this prohibition, that is, it was held improper for two persons to be joined in marriage who were not permitted to speak each other's names.

Women, especially young women, seldom spoke the names of their husbands, but many of the old women did not hesitate to do so. When it was necessary for a woman to speak of her husband, if she had children she would say, "This child's father," or "My child's father." Neither men nor women liked to tell their own names.

Polygamy was not general among the Dakotas, a single wife being the rule, and polygamy the exception. Among the Medawakantonwan less than one tenth, and perhaps not more than one twentieth, had more than one wife at a time, in remarkable contrast with the polygamy which Julius Caesar described as prevailing among our British ancestors.

The extent to which polygamy generally existed among the Dakotas at any time depended upon the relative number of men and women. If the number of the men was about equal to that of the women, not many of them would have more than one wife, for very few would live without wives. But if many of the men should have been lost in battle or in any other way, so that their number should not nearly equal that of the women, polygamy would prevail just in proportion to the lack of men, for few of the women would live long unmarried. Polygamy was not popular with the Dakotas, and they generally spoke of it as undesirable, but it existed more or less in every band.

The wives of a polygamist could seldom live together in peace, and if a man were to take more than one wife, it was thought best to marry sisters because they were less likely to quarrel than women between whom there were no ties of blood relationship. Few Indian women would have been reconciled to polygamy if it had not been for the great help women were to each other, especially when on the hunting expeditions.

The Dakotas, both men and women, learned to maintain on almost all occasions an appearance of stoical apathy. We could not expect lovers among them to be very demonstrative, but evidently many husbands and wives were very much attached to each other. The attachment of some, however, if they had any, did not last long. It was not an uncommon thing for married persons to separate after living together a short time. These separations were sometimes final, but often the husband returned after a short absence. The young husband frequently left his wife, not because he was dissatisfied with her, but because he disliked her relatives or was homesick, for the husband and wife often belonged to different villages. Separations and reconciliations might be repeated several times, and finally the parties might live together permanently. If they did not forsake each other utterly before they had homes and families of their own, they were likely to live together till death separated them.

Social and Industrial Condition of Women.

The women were often abused and had hard service to perform, but neither wives nor daughters were treated as slaves. They had their acknowledged rights, and spirit to maintain them. In many respects they were treated by the men as equals, and participated with them in their most solemn religious festivals. They had no voice in the public councils, but they contrived to make themselves heard at home, and I have known them to remove a camp in spite of the remonstrances of the men. In theory, each man ruled in his own house (or rather family, for the house belonged to the woman); and this theory was carried out in practice about as well as it is with their white neighbors. The wife did not break her promise to obey her husband, for she never made any vows to either break or keep; but he was as likely to be ruled by her as she by him. In an actual fight between husband and wife, he was pretty sure to come off conqueror, for, if she was too strong for him, he seized his weapons of war; but their quarrels did not always proceed to blows, and in a war of words she was at least a match for him. If she was not able to fight with him, she had a great many ways of convincing him that it was best for him to keep the peace with her. It required but a slight acquaintance with the Dakotas, to discover that, as a general thing, the women were not afraid of their husbands. Indeed, Dakota women, old or young, are not the right material to be made slaves.

It is true that the women were feminine in their disposition. Squaws are not generally amazons or furies. With rare exceptions, they are not masculine in their dispositions, habits, or aspirations. Very few of them manifest any inclination to meddle with fire-arms or other weapons, even when it may seem necessary, or to engage in hunting, trapping, or fishing. Girls show no disposition to play with bows and arrows, and, though I have seen them fishing from necessity, they seemed to take no delight in it. They were indefatigable in their search for wild berries and other wild fruits, but to the wild game they gave little attention till it was laid down at their doors. The women were always armed with knives, and, if attacked, doubtless defended themselves as well as they could: but they were always women, and, when frightened, obeyed the natural instincts of the sex and shrieked for help. Even the language spoken by the women differed from that of the men, so that by reading a single sentence of a letter one can tell whether it was written by a male or a female. In a word, the difference in disposition and habits, between men and women, was as great among Indians as among us.

But though the women differed from the men, they were not held in subjection by them. Though feminine, they were not imbecile in body or mind. Hardened by the exercise of their rude labors, and armed with fortitude and resolution, they did not tamely submit to what they considered unjust treatment. The woman was acknowledged owner of the tent and nearly all that was in it. Her husband might desert her and take his gun and traps along with him, but he could not turn her out of the house, or take her children from her if they chose to stay with her. She might be left in destitute circumstances, but her neighbors would not suffer her nor her children to starve.

Young women, when first married, were usually for a considerable time, frequently for several years, under the protection of their parents and brothers and sisters, and the husband was perhaps as much in danger of being abused by them as was the wife by him. Some women were so maltreated by their brutal husbands that they were greatly to be pitied, and some husbands were so treated by their wives that they were not greatly to be envied; but perhaps such things are hardly worth mentioning, for they are not Indian peculiarities.

TREATMENT AND EDUCATION OF CHILDREN.

Parents did not commonly treat either their sons or their daughters harshly, and both boys and girls were taught to cultivate a self-reliant, independent spirit.

Infants were very tenderly cared for. They were wrapped in bandages and laid on the little board cradle that has been mentioned. A bandage of woolen cloth was wound around them and the cradle, holding the baby firmly in its place. A veil or curtain was fastened to the top of the cradle and hung down to the foot, being kept from the child's face by a wooden bow. The veil protected the child's face from the wind, cold, sunshine, dust, insects, etc. The bow also served to protect the child in case of an accidental fall. The feet rested on a projection, but the babe while very young was supported chiefly by the bandages around it. The cradle was carried on the back, supported by a strap which rested on the head of the bearer, and it needed no rocking.

Nothing better than this cradle could have been contrived for the comfort and safety of the infants. There was no other way in which they could be carried on the frequent journeys with safety. They were taken from the cradle often enough to give them exercise, and most mothers took great pains to keep them clean. The cradle was carved and painted, and its trappings were sometimes very highly ornamented, a woman sometimes spending weeks embroidering the wrappings of her child.

There was no efficient family government among the Dakotas, and severe measures were seldom resorted to for the maintenance of parental authority. The parents gave advice to their children, but fathers did not often lay their commands upon them. When they wished their children to perform any service, they usually spoke kindly to them, saying, "My son, or my daughter, will you do this?" Generally in their intercourse with their children there was a mildness of manner such as we would hardly expect to find among savages.

Some parents had great influence over their children, and others very little. Some possessed and others lacked those personal qualities which command respect and obedience. They always commended an obedient disposition, and were pleased to have their children docile and good-natured, but they did not approve of subduing the spirit of a child by force and compelling him to submit to authority. Fathers rarely, if ever, inflicted corporal punishment on their children. The mothers chastised them only when so provoked as to lose all command over their temper. They might sometimes be seen chasing their refractory sons through a village and throwing sticks at them, but such ebullitions of passion were not of very frequent occurrence.

Nothing seemed to provoke fathers to use harsh language toward their sons so much as to observe in them indications of effeminacy or cowardice. Among their traditionary tales is the following. When most of the men of a certain village were about starting on a war expedition, one young man who did not seem inclined to go was sharply reproved by his father, who said to him, "I suppose you hope to have a good time with the women when the men are all gone." The son, stung by his father's reproaches, joined the war party; but the Ojibways were found securely posted on an inaccessible island, and the party were compelled to return without accomplishing anything. As they were about to turn back, the young man handed one of his garments to a comrade, saying, "Make my father sad with this;" then plunging into the lake, he swam to the island and was killed by the enemy.

I once lived three months in the tepee of Whistling Wind, a man well known to the old traders as one of the most industrious and successful fur-hunters. He had a nephew living with him, who spent more time than his uncle thought necessary in oiling his hair. One day, while he was engaged in smoothing his locks with deer's marrow, I heard Whistling Wind say to him sharply, "Nephew, when I was young, we oiled our feet and said, 'My feet be swift in the chase,' but you neglect your feet and put the oil on your head."

Mention has been made of Red Bird, who was killed in an attack on the Mille Lacs Indians. That expedition was undertaken to avenge the death of a son-in-law of his sister. As Red Bird was about to start after the Ojibways, he saw his oldest son, a boy of fifteen or sixteen years of age, weeping over the dead body, and said to him, "Why are you crying like a woman? Don't you know which way the Ojibways have gone?" The boy took the hint, and, following his father, was mortally wounded by a shot in the abdomen. After he was wounded he called for his father, and when the bystanders asked what he wished he pointed to the wound and said, "I want my father to see this. I suppose it is what he wanted." When told that his father was dead, he did not speak again.

Children, in return for the kindness received from their parents, usually evinced much regard for them, taking care of them in their old age. It is perhaps unnecessary to say that some parents neglected their children, and that some children were ungrateful to their parents.

The young were often admonished to treat the aged with deference, and these admonitions were in some measure regarded. The aged and experienced were accounted wiser than the young, and their opinions given in council had great weight. The wisdom of age was held in higher esteem than with us, and this may be attributed to the fact that what they knew of the past they learned from the aged, while our young people learn from books.

Great pains were taken to educate their sons in the hunter's craft, and both boys and girls had much to learn to fit them for their station in life, low as that station seemed to be. It is quite as easy to learn to get a living by farming as by hunting where game is as scarce as it was in the country of the Dakotas, and ignorance and stupidity are as great disqualifications for the hunter or warrior as for the mechanic.

Daughters had a great many lessons to take before their education was completed, for, though they appeared to us to know almost nothing, they knew a great deal of which we are ignorant, and it was to them useful knowledge, essential to their welfare. No one could be long with the Dakotas without hearing them give their children such instruction as would qualify them to take care of themselves.

Whatever they did or made, it was the aim of the Dakotas to do everything well and in a workmanlike manner, if it was nothing more than making a moccasin, a ramrod, or a paddle for a canoe.

They did not like to be thought bunglers, or to see their children, either boys or girls, do anything awkwardly.

There were a great many things to be learned about the habits of wild animals and birds, the best manner of approaching them, handling fire-arms so as to avoid accidents, setting traps, etc. They took much pains to learn to imitate the voices of birds and beasts, and this was a very necessary part of the education of both the hunter and the warrior. When near an enemy they could communicate with each other by mimicking the voice of birds, without giving alarm; and they sometimes imposed upon the beasts which they were hunting by counterfeiting the voice of the mother or her young. They had discovered a great many ways of accomplishing their purposes, which none but a race of practical hunters would ever have thought of.

I was once walking through scattering trees and bushes, with a man who had a bow and arrows. He shot one of the arrows at a humming-bird which he discovered near by. We searched for the arrow some time in vain, and, as he stopped looking for it, I supposed he had given it up for lost; but he went back, and, placing himself where he stood when he discharged the first arrow, he shot another, watching carefully where it fell. He then found them both without any difficulty. Probably his attention was so completely given to the humming-bird that he did not watch the flight of the first arrow, but he knew how to find it.

They took special pains to teach their children how to guard against being frozen, and the young people profited well by these instructions, so that notwithstanding their exposures it was a rare thing for a sober Dakota to be seriously injured by the frost. With their fire-steel and flint, they would kindle fires when anyone but an Indian would have thought it an impossibility, and it was well that they could do it, for often the preservation of their lives depended on the speedy starting of a fire under the most difficult circumstances.

In the winter of 1835-36, I left a camp of hunters on Rum river, near the border of the Ojibway country, to come alone to Lake Calhoun. As it was midwinter and I was coming without any track across a region of country I had never seen, I knew the Indians would protest against it, and therefore said nothing about my purpose till I was ready to start. When I went to take leave of the chief, he remonstrated against the proposed journey, deeming it a foolhardy undertaking for a white man, as doubtless it was. Seeing that I could not be moved from my purpose, he said to me very seriously, "You white men are wise, but we have some maxims about traveling in winter, which we consider of great importance, and if you will go I want to give you a little advice before you start. Do not trust the ice on the river until you have thoroughly examined it, and take good care of your hands and feet. If you freeze your hands you cannot build a fire, and if you freeze your feet you cannot walk."

The Indians were so much concerned about me on that occasion, that the chief sent his brother to overtake me and accompany me home. He told me afterward, that he followed me half a day, but found my steps so long that he despaired of overtaking me, and, after staying out one night, returned to camp.

PERSONAL NAMES.

The Dakotas have ten common names for children, which they inherit as a birthright, five for males and five for females, so that each of the first five children in a family is provided with a name as soon as it is born. The firstborn, if a son, is called Chaska, and if a daughter, Winona, and so of the other eight names. These names indicate the sex and the order of time in which the children are born; but only five of such names could belong to the same family. If a family consisted of more than that number, the younger ones had to be provided with other names.

It might happen that a child was the firstborn of one parent and not of the other, and in that case it was generally counted according to the place it held in the family of the mother, but might be counted with the children of either parent. These names were very convenient, and parents often continued to call their children by them long after they were known by other names.

Almost all children had other names given them, and in most cases while they were still very young. The first bird that a boy killed with an arrow, though no larger than a wren, was cooked and some man was invited to eat it and to give the boy a name; but that name might be changed for another when he killed an enemy if not before. The meaning of the names given was some-

times obvious enough, but many of them had an occult signification and needed to be interpreted by those who gave them. The
names of females were distinguished from the names of males by
a difference of termination, and were such as were considered appropriate to females.

When young men signalized themselves by some act of bravery,
they were honored by having the name of some celebrated ancestor
bestowed upon them. Names that are mentioned by white men who
very long ago visited the Dakotas are still common among them,
and probably the same names have been in use for many centuries.
Men might change or try to change their names at any time, and
some were known by more than one name.

As the Dakotas depended chiefly on their relatives for protection and defence, they were careful to know and acknowledge their
kindred to a very remote degree, but their chief reliance was on
those who were nearly related to them. They expected their brothers,
cousins, uncles, and nephews, to stand by them in case of necessity,
and this expectation was not often disappointed. Whatever differ-
ences these relatives might have among themselves, they were ready
to support each other in case of need against all others. It was
well understood that one who had many and powerful relatives,
however weak he might be himself, could not be injured or insulted
with impunity.

The Dakota method of reckoning kindred differs from ours,
but it would take too many words to explain the difference. Many
who are called by us uncles and aunts, are called by them fathers
and mothers; so that many who are cousins with us are brothers
and sisters with them, and some whom we call nephews and nieces
they call sons and daughters. They have many names denoting
different degrees of relationship, which we comprehend under the
general head of cousins or distant relatives.

ADULTERY AND FORNICATION.

As matrimony has been spoken of, it may be thought that
something should be said about the manner in which the marriage
covenant was kept, but it is difficult to know just what to say on
such a subject as this. Adultery was condemned among the Dakotas by public opinion, and was sometimes severely punished;
consequently, when committed, it was a secret crime. Unfaithful-

ness in a married woman was considered deserving of the severest punishment, and such punishment was sometimes inflicted. The husband would also have been justified by public opinion in avenging himself on his wife's paramour, even to the shedding of his blood. Under such circumstances, the perpetrators of this crime would ordinarily be careful to guard against detection, so that it would be as presumptuous for any writer to undertake to tell how much or how little adultery prevailed among the Dakotas, as for him to pretend to know how much of it there is in St. Paul or Chicago.

We know that there was a looseness of morals among this people, but to what extent it prevailed none can tell with certainty. Because some were known to be dissolute, to condemn all the rest on mere suspicion, to condemn a multitude of women who were never suspected by their own husbands, would be unfair.

Let us not slander them even though they were heathen women, and though most of them are now in their graves where calumny can do them no harm. I have no high opinion of the chastity of the Dakotas, male or female; but with the consideration of the circumstances in which the women were placed, they certainly deserve credit for what virtue they did have. To condemn them in such sweeping terms as have been used by respectable writers when speaking of the women of southern Europe, would be unjust. If the women of France, Spain, and Italy, are not shamefully slandered by writers who are supposed to be men of veracity, the Dakota women were more virtuous than they.

It is probable that adultery was not rare among the Dakotas. Some men suspected their wives and watched them, and some of them doubtless needed watching; but I believe a large majority of Dakota women were never suspected of unfaithfulness by those who knew them best. There were a great many families reared by them, of whom no one could have any reasonable doubt that they were all children of the same father and mother.

While adultery was reprobated by popular sentiment, unchastity in the unmarried was not in good repute. The loss of a reputation for virtue was, perhaps, as great a loss to the Indian girl as it is to the white girl; and while no one acquainted with them believes that they were all virtuous, it is almost certain that many of them were not licentious. If it were proper, remarkable examples could be given of the prudery of some, and the shamelessness of others. Some were lascivious, having as little regard for appearances as some of their white sisters, while others were very careful of their reputation, never going alone where there was danger of their being suspected of improper conduct.

During a residence among them of about twenty years, I never knew an Indian girl, while living among her own people, to give birth to a child before she was married. Compare this fact with the crowded foundling hospitals of some civilized countries. But to esteem all the unmarried girls chaste would be to have a better opinion of some of them than they had of themselves.

Tacit confession of guilt was sometimes extorted from them by a certain ordeal through which they were compelled to pass. The Dakotas had a custom of making a feast, occasionally, to which all were invited who had not been guilty of a breach of the laws of chastity. The feast was sometimes for the married, and sometimes for the unmarried. The guests all sat in a circle on the ground, both males and females being invited. Those who were conscious of disqualifying conduct were warned not to partake of the feast, lest the gods should be offended and some evil befall them; and that was not the only danger to which they were exposed, for it was the duty of any who were cognizant of their guilt to remove them from the circle. To stay away was to confess their guilt, and to participate in the feast was to run the risk not only of public exposure but of offending the gods.

At the feast for the unmarried I never saw any men except very young ones, but nearly all the unmarried young women were there. Some, however, staid away. With the unmarried it was probably a pretty severe test of character, for if any attended the feast who had no right to it there could be little danger in exposing them; but I do not think much could be learned from this test in regard to the character of married persons.

If a man had illicit intercourse with the wife of his neighbor, he would be in no haste to make the fact public, and a woman might fear the wrath of her husband more than the anger of the gods. I have known but two removals from the ring, one of a married woman, which caused much excitement, and the other of an unmarried girl. They, however, both protested that they were innocent.

I have mentioned this trial feast as a curious custom of the Dakotas, and as throwing some light on the character of this people. It proves that they thought chastity and conjugal fidelity worth guarding, and such a custom was not likely to be adopted or observed by a people sunk to the lowest depths of licentiousness. Let us be thankful that we have no such pagan customs and are not subject, as these dark-minded heathen were, to such annoying and impertinent inquisitions.

As for prostitutes, they were held in no higher estimation among the Dakotas than among white Americans. Their occupation was not so profitable as that of the same class of persons among their civilized neighbors, for they had all the disgrace of the vocation with none of its rewards except insult and contumely. The name of harlot was the most opprobrious epithet that could be bestowed on an Indian woman. There was no encouragement for such persons, unless they were patronized by white men; and there were few women who did not live with their husbands, excepting widows and those who had been divorced.

Of the manners of the females in public we can speak with more confidence than of their conduct in private. As a general rule they were chaste in their conversation and modest in their behavior, both at home and abroad. Many of the young women were diffident and bashful and very much afraid they should say or do something unbecoming. Mothers took great pains in training their daughters to habits of decorum. They were taught to assume the correct posture when sitting, and to gather their garments closely around their feet. I have heard little girls sharply reprimanded by their mothers for the careless exposure of their persons.

It is true that the mode of life of the Dakotas did not permit such habits of privacy as prevail among the civilized. Scores of women and girls might be seen swimming in rivers and lakes, at least their heads might be seen; but they did not bathe in company with the men, like the ancient Teutons, as described by Caesar. They sought retired places when such could be found, but nothing could keep them out of the water in warm weather; and it was better that they should bathe in public places than that they should not bathe at all.

All Dakotas, both men and women, were accustomed to hear and use expressions of language that would not be tolerated in civilized society, but they used such language less than might have been naturally expected. Many words, the use of which is interdicted among us, were used by them without any suspicion of their impropriety, saying in plain words what we express in indirect terms; but when one became accustomed to the words, he thought little of their impropriety, for they suggested no other ideas than do the phrases which we use as substitutes for them.

Euphemisms were by no means unknown among the Dakotas, and many were careful to avoid whatever language they considered indelicate. Some of the women were very particular in this respect, while others, especially the older ones, were less guarded in their conversation, and some of the men were exceedingly vile. They were the most likely to use filthy language in the presence of some vile white man, who set them the example and seemed best pleased with them when their language was the most exceptionable. Many of them could accommodate themselves to the company they were in. To the dissolute white man they would show their worst side, and to one of an opposite character their best side, so that both were liable to be deceived. To one they appeared worse than they really were, and to the other better.

There was one thing which, more than any other, led some persons to form an unjust estimate of the general character of the Dakota woman. When a white man became known to the Indians as a man of doubtful character he came chiefly in contact with the worst specimens of female character. Only the lewd cared to have anything to do with him, and all others carefully avoided him.

If we wished to know the character of American women for chastity, should we inquire of those whose intercourse with them is confined to the most lascivious and licentious? Yet it is from such persons that the public gets most of its information concerning the character of Dakota women. Many of them would not go where they were likely to meet one of our soldiers without an escort to protect them from insult. A great many of the more respectable of the Indian women seldom went near the house of a white man, except when it was necessary, but staid at home and industriously engaged in taking care of their families. The conversation of many of the Indians was lewd enough at best, but probably the worst language that some of the women ever heard was addressed to them by white men. Yet I do not think the example of the whites had, up to the year 1834, exerted a very deleterious influence on the Dakotas as a people.

The character of some of the females in the vicinity of Fort Snelling suffered in consequence of their intercourse with soldiers and others, but they were few in comparison with the mass of the people, and their example was not thought worthy of imitation. A great many of the women in the neighborhood of the fort, however, had nothing to do with unprincipled white men; while those living more remote seldom saw any white man but the traders, who commonly each had an Indian wife of his own.

Whatever may be thought of the conduct of officers and others, who cohabited with Indian women, as far as the women themselves were concerned it was lawful wedlock. They were married according to the customs of their people, and were wives, not concubines.

While some of the whites were exerting a bad influence over the Indians, others gave them salutary advice and set them good examples. I should have thought that the example of the whites had done the Indians much damage, if I had not had an opportunity to compare those nearest the white people with those more remote from them. In 1834, the morals of the former were certainly as good as those of the latter, and they were more intelligent and more agreeable in their manners. In later years, however, they were rapidly demoralized by coming into too close contact with their white neighbors.

In concluding what I have to say about the chastity or unchastity of the Dakotas, I will only add that while all who knew them will admit that they were quite bad enough, yet when we consider that their libidinous passions had no restraint but the private conscience of pagans and the public sentiment of a savage people, ignorant of all religious obligations, and that the marriage contract had no legal force, we may well wonder that we found among them so many families, so many men and women living together as man and wife, whom nothing but death could separate, and who used their best endeavors to take care of their children, make them comfortable, and place them in a position to take care of themselves when they could do no more for them.

CLEANLINESS.

All who write about Indians characterize them as filthy, and if they mean by this term that their mode of life is such that they cannot keep themselves as clean as those who live in houses, have changes of raiment, and conveniences for washing and bathing, it is true; but if they mean to say that they are reconciled to filth and take no pains to keep thmselves clean, it is a mistake, at least so far as the Dakotas are concerned.

Certainly they kept neither their persons nor their garments clean, not always so clean as they might, and it would have been strange if they had not become so accustomed to soiled garments as not to be very much shocked at the sight of them. Huddled together in little tents a great portion of the year, without soap or other conveniences for washing, having no change of clothing, and often compelled to wear the same garments by night and by day, they could not present a neat and tidy appearance. The question is not whether they were clean, but whether they were as cleanlv as they well could be under such circumstances, that is, as cleanly as they could be and support themselves by hunting.

I have heard a white woman, who was intimately acquainted with the habits of the Indian women, say that she did not believe any white woman, situated as they were, would keep herself as clean as most of them did. That filthy and squalid appearance which Indians often presented to the eyes of a white man, was a necessity of their manner of life, unavoidable so long as they lived by the chase.

It would be as reasonable to declaim against the smut on the face of a coal miner, as against the dirty appearance of Indians. If they wore any garments, they must wear soiled ones. They were too poor to own, and were unable to carry on their journeys, such clothing, bedding, and washing apparatus, as were necessary to secure personal cleanliness.

The overloaded women could not carry a washtub in their removals, and considered even a wash-basin an incumbrance; so, instead of using one, they drew the water into their mouths and spirted it out into their hands and thus washed their hands and faces. This was a heathenish fashion, but better than none. In fact there was no place in the little crowded tent in which to use a wash-basin, and we could hardly expect even a Dakota to wash outdoors in the winter.

When I accompanied a winter hunting party, this matter of washing was rather embarrassing after the lakes and streams were frozen over. I was notified, by the mistress of the house, that all washing at the common watering place was strictly interdicted. There was no washbowl or basin, and, if I washed in any dish or kettle, it would be perpetually polluted and could never again be used for cooking purposes, for these filthy Indians have some very strict notions. I did not like to go to a distance of twenty or thirty rods and cut a hole through the ice every time I wished to wash myself, neither did I fancy their mode of washing. Therefore I washed in the snow, and doubtless they inferred from it that I was whimsical, more whimsical than wise. In the meantime my clothing could not be washed in the snow, so I stood it as well as I could, and threw my under-garments into the last fire kindled on my way home. The Indians could not afford to purify their raiment by fire, and probably I should not have done so had I not at that time been somewhat of a novice.

In reading vivid accounts of the filthy and disgusting appearance of Indians, I can hardly help wishing that the writers were compelled to take a nearer view of them and live with them, faring as they do, through just one winter's campaign. I should like to see which came out the cleaner in the spring, the white man or the Indian.

When the white lady looked on the soiled blanket and greasy coat of the Indian woman, she was shocked at her filthy appearance, as she well might be. She pronounced her a filthy wretch, and yet very likely that filthy creature had been into the cold water of some lake or river up to her waist once a month all winter, to wash herself and her clothing. For this purpose, they went into deep springs when they could find them; but if they could get at the water in no other way, they cut holes through the ice. They went in with their clothes on, and built fires on the shore by which they stood and dried themselves and their garments. These ablutions were performed in the coldest winter weather, when it made one shiver to think of it. Is it fair for those who have their warm rooms and warm baths, to stigmatize these heroic women as filthy wretches?

In the summer all but the aged bathed often, and they also washed their garments in the lakes and streams.

SWIMMING.

In swimming, the Dakota men used their feet and legs much in the manner of frogs, as white people ordinarily do, but they did not strike with both hands at a time. They used their hands alternately, and, while striking with one, raised the other out of the water and reached forward. Their alternate use of the hands gave their heads and shoulders a rolling motion, as they turned first on one side, then on the other. They could not swim quite so rapidly as if they had used both hands at once, but could swim farther, as in our usual way the arms tire sooner than the lower limbs. In their mode of swimming they struck but half as many blows with their hands as with their feet, one arm resting while the other was in use; and, by lifting their hands out of the water, they avoided the resistance ordinarily encountered in moving them forward.

The women, who in everything they did had a fashion of their own, differing from that of the men, used their arms as white people commonly do, but their feet they held near together, and, raising them alternately out of the water, propelled themselves by striking backward with the top of the foot against the water. These blows with the feet they struck in rapid succession, and when many of them were swimming together they made more noise than the paddle wheels of a steamboat.

DISEASES.

The Dakotas do not seem to possess remarkably strong constitutions, as compared with white people; but it is not easy to draw a comparison of this kind between nations differing so much in their condition and mode of life. It is difficult to know how much of their sickness and disease was owing to debility of constitution, and how large a portion of it should be attributed to hardship, exposure, unwholesome diet, etc.

One who only saw a company of Dakotas and observed their healthy, robust look, especially that of the women, was likely to form an erroneous opinion concerning their general health and strength of constitution. These hardy looking men and women were only a remnant who had outlived a multitude of their companions, as a few of the strongest trees may be left standing in a forest through which a hurricane has passed.

Among civilized people, the lives of the feeble, sickly, and helpless, may be long preserved by proper care and attention, but such persons cannot long endure the vicissitudes of savage life. The reason why the Dakotas did not increase faster was not because so few were born, but because so many died. I kept for a time the record of births in one village, and am confident that the number was greater than is common among an equal number of white people. This would be natural, for almost every marriageable woman lived with a husband, and they all rejoiced in the increase of their families. The Indian women were at least as prolific as the generality of women, and when married to white men, and living in comfortable circumstances, they generally raised large families of children; but death was always busy thinning out the Indian families, and when they arrived at middle age only a few of them were left. Some were killed by their enemies and others died of starvation, but these were few compared with those who died of diseases. By far the larger part died in infancy and childhood. Parents tried to take good care of their children, but they could not always protect them from the inclemency of the weather; often they had no suitable food for them at weaning time, or when they were sick; and many of them were carried off by the diseases to which children are everywhere liable.

In the spring of 1847, about thirty children died of the whooping-cough at Shakopee, most of them infants, and constituting not far from one-twentieth of the population.

Except the diseases incident to infancy and childhood, the Dakotas suffered more perhaps from scrofula and consumption than from any other diseases. About the year 1850, bilious diseases prevailed to an alarming extent all along the Mississippi and Minnesota rivers, and many of the Indians died from the effects of the epidemic complaints. About 1834, a great portion of the Wabashaw band died of smallpox, and that disease has since proved fatal to some of the Dakotas, but its ravages have been greatly checked by vaccination. Notwithstanding there was so much of sickness and death among the Dakotas, their numbers did not seem to be diminishing while they lived by hunting.

Dr. T. S. Williamson, who resided many years at Lac qui Parle, said that the number of Indians in that vicinity was slowly increasing; and the same was probably true of most of the bands within the limits of Minnesota. The race did not by any means appear to be a worn-out race on the verge of extinction, but a strong and vigorous one, in mind and body. If white men had not crossed the track of this people, I know not why it might not have continued to exist through thousands of years to come. They had encountered and survived as many hardships and difficulties in the past as they were likely to meet in the future, and they exhibited no signs of degeneracy which unfitted them for taking care of themselves as well as their ancestors had done before them.

The reader will bear in mind that I am describing the Dakotas as we found them, not as they have become since we have tried on them an experiment in the way of civilization. Without cultivating the soil, they never could have been much more numerous than they were unless they had enlarged their territory by seizing on the lands of their neighbors, for there were as many of them as their country would support while they lived by hunting. This is the true reason why the Indian population did not increase.

INSANITY.

I have seen but one insane Dakota, except in cases of temporary insanity caused by fevers. The insane person mentioned had been the wife of a Canadian, and after she lost her reason had no certain home, depending upon charity for support. When I have seen her, she was well clothed and seemed to be well fed; but I do not know what finally became of her.

Many years ago a woman became insane in consequence of having been with a hunting party which was reduced to such a state of starvation that the sufferers ate the bodies of their companions. After her return, she would look at the children who were fleshy and remark that they were good to eat, and once, seeing some pumpkins, she said she wished they were men's heads.

The Indians of the village to which she belonged, fearing that she would kill some of them, put her across the Minnesota river, and as she swam back in the night killed her with clubs when she reached the shore. I received the account from some who helped to kill her, and suppose the occurrence took place about the year 1820.

About 1845, a girl eight or ten years of age was tied in a tent, being left to die there alone, by the Indians of Oak Grove, because she was deranged. I found her before she was quite dead, but not in time to save her life. Her parents had recently died, and she had no relatives at that place. All the principal men of the village approved of the deed, saying they were afraid she would do mischief. Probably she would not have been killed, certainly she would have been spared longer, if she had had relatives to take care of her, for she had been insane only a few weeks.

Cases of confirmed insanity must have been rare among the Dakotas, for I can recollect only these which have been mentioned, though doubtless there were others.

If an insane person had relatives and was harmless, probably he was taken care of as idiots were; but, if considered dangerous, he was killed or left to perish, for he could not be confined.

DEFORMITY AND IDIOCY.

I have known but few badly deformed Dakotas, and I saw nearly all the men and women who lived on the Mississippi and Minnesota rivers at the period from 1834 to 1840. The worst deformed Indian I ever saw was idiotic and nearly helpless, yet she was well taken care of and lived until nearly grown.

The only idiots I have known among the Dakotas were related to each other. The girl who has been mentioned, as having been both deformed and idiotic, had a cousin who was an idiot, but he was well cared for and lived to grow up to manhood. He never learned to talk, and was accidentally drowned. It is doubtful whether, as a general rule, great pains would be taken to preserve the lives of badly deformed or idiotic children; and even if taken care of, they would not be likely to live long, for none have more need of sound minds and active bodies than they who live by the chase.

The Indians were very much ashamed of any personal deformity, and took all possible pains to conceal it. A man who had lost his hand or part of it by the bursting of a gun would hide the defect as much as possible, keeping it wrapped in his blanket.

A young man of my acquaintance, who had lost one hand by the bursting of a gun, was an active and successful hunter, and could dress a deer as well as those who had two hands. I asked one of his brothers how he did it, but he said he did not know. No one had ever seen him do it. It was supposed that he used his teeth, but he would never dress a deer in the presence of others.

I once heard a one-eyed orator make a speech at the Agency house, who kept his blind eye carefully covered with the hair of his head. Often during his speech he put his hand to his eye, to assure himself that it was not exposed.

SURGERY AND MEDICINE.

The Dakotas did not perform many surgical operations. They practiced bleeding to a considerable extent, both by scarifying and opening veins. Some of them were very successful in the treatment of wounds. They were very careful to keep the wound clean and well dressed, and used with success certain plants and roots in reducing swellings and removing inflammation.

As among other people, so likewise among the Dakotas, there were two systems of medicine or modes of treating the sick. One was founded in reason and was the result of experience, and was the same in its nature as that adopted by the great mass of the civilized world; the other was supported by no reason, but was the invention of cunning imposters, who for their own profit pretended to cure diseases by the exercise of powers which they themselves knew they did not possess. These two systems of treatment were entirely dissimilar, and had no connection with each other.

Sometimes the sick Indian was healed by the use of appropriate medicines, and sometimes he paid the conjurer or wakanman for shaking his rattle over his head. The professed conjurers had no more conscience than the clairvoyants, spiritualists, and other quacks, who practice on the superstitious credulity of the white people. They were very numerous and had great influence over the people, but it is a mistake to suppose that the Dakotas depended solely on the wakan-men for the removal of diseases.

They believed in the efficacy of medicines and made great use of them.

For external injuries they made external application of such things as they had learned to value through experience, and for internal diseases they administered medicines as we do. They had learned the medicinal qualities of a great many plants, roots, etc., which they held in high estimation; but they soon discovered that many of their remedies were inferior to those in possession of the whites, and made frequent application to us for medicines.

About the year 1847, when many of the Indians at Shakopee and Carver were sick, I had forty applications for medicines in one day, and at the same time there was very little conjuration over the sick. Not one in twenty called the wakan-men for help, but depended entirely on the healing power of medicine for recovery.

I have said that there was no connection between the use of medicines and conjuration. There might seem to be, for conjurers used medicines as well as others, and some of them were quite skillful in the use of them; but if they administered medicines, that was a separate matter and was done for extra pay. No doubt they often contrived to have their incantations credited with cures that were actually wrought by medicines.

Some who were not conjurers understood the nature of medicines as well as they did and knew as well how to administer them. Some had, or pretended to have, valuable medicines which they sold for high prices, but the proprietors of these medicines were not all wakan-men.

The theory adopted by the wakan-men was that internal diseases were caused by some malignant supernatural influence, consequently that superhuman aid must be invoked to effect their removal; and in attempting to induce Satan to cast out Satan they made strange work of it. When a person was so sick as to need the aid of one of these doctors, a messenger was sent to him with a present or the promise of one, and if he thought the reward sufficient he immediately waited on the patient. The doctor pretended to know the cause of the disease, and sometimes whether it could be cured. This knowledge he obtained from the invisible world, and he had the advantage in this respect of some of our own impostors, for he did not need to examine anything taken from the body of the patient, not even a lock of hair. The disease was commonly ascribed to some transgression, intentional or accidental, of some one of their superstitious rules.

To prepare for the operations of the conjurer, a tent was pitched or one was vacated, and the sick person was laid on his back in the tent, with his breast bared. The doctor then stood over him, shaking his gourd-seed rattle, and uttering the most horrible sounds of which the human voice is capable. These utterances were accompanied with stamping and violent contortions of his body. From time to time, the conjurer applied his mouth to the body of the patient, and with much ado and a great deal of noise pretended to draw out the disease by suction, spitting frequently into a dish and examining carefully the color of the saliva, which was commonly tinged with red or blue. This tinge must have been caused by some coloring substance held in the mouth, but he represented that it was caused by the disease and varied according to the nature of the malady. The sounds emitted by the operator were the most disagreeable that I ever heard, and his whole appearance the most revolting of anything to be seen among the Dakotas. If the patient lived, the physician had the credit of curing him; and if, on the other hand, he died, there were ways enough to account for his death, without ascribing it to the unskillfulness of the doctor.

There were many of these conjurers, some of them women, but much the larger number were men. They were a brazen-faced set of impostors, who practiced deception because they found it profitable to do so, for they did not work without good pay. We wonder sometimes how the Indians could have been deceived by them, and yet I have lately known some of my intelligent white neighbors to employ a spiritualist physician, who claimed to have learned how to treat diseases from the ghost of one of these old Indian doctors. If white men can believe in a dead Indian, why should not Dakotas believe in a live one? If a living dog is better than a dead lion, surely a live Indian should be better than a dead one.

BURIAL CUSTOMS AND MOURNING.

As soon as a person had died, or while he was dying, his friends dressed him in the best clothes they could procure, putting embroidered moccasins on his feet, and when he was dead they wrapped the body in a blanket made fast by bandages wound around it. Often many blankets and other cloths were wrapped around, one over another. A coffin was procured if possible, generally from some white man. We made many for them, and they were required to be very large to contain the body with all the clothing that was wrapped around it. Some were buried when they died, but most of them were placed for a time on trees or scaffolds. In the region of the upper Minnesota river, I have seen them wrapped in buffalo-skins and fastened among the branches of trees, and it is not probable that the Dakotas used coffins before they were acquainted with white men. At Lac qui Parle, I have known one or two dead bodies to be left on trees until the enwrapping buffalo-skins decayed and the bones fell to the earth. These were, however, rare cases of neglect, for it was the custom of the Dakotas to bury their dead either immediately or within a few weeks or months after death.

When a white man first saw the Dakotas' dead bodies lying on trees or scaffolds, he was shocked at such a barbarous practice, and, if he was a superficial observer, could see no reason to justify it and attributed the practice to the degraded, brutish nature of the Indians. But if he was an observing, thoughtful man, and examined the matter attentively, the custom would soon appear to him in a new light. In forming an opinion of the habits and practices of the Dakotas, we should bear in mind what we know of their past history and former condition, before they had any acquaintance with civilized people or any tools excepting those of their own manufacture. We should also remember that the customs of a people, once adopted from necessity, are likely to be continued after the necessity for them ceases to exist. Practices that are now out of place might have been proper a hundred years ago, but it would have been strange if the Dakotas had not retained some of the customs of their ancestors longer than there was any real necessity for their observance.

We are to remember that the Dakotas have always inhabited a cold country, and that they had no tools for digging except what they made for themselves. Under such circumstances, it would have been an utter impossibility for them to dig graves in the winter, and they could preserve the bodies of their dead from wild beasts only by placing them on trees or scaffolds. It was not laziness nor indifference that prevented their digging graves, for when their friends died during hunting expeditions, far from home, they would carry their dead bodies a hundred miles or more to lay them beside their kindred. They did not carry them in wagons or cars, but with their own hands, making biers like the litters for the wounded which have been described. On these rude biers they brought home their dead, often wading with them through deep snows several days' journey. They would be the last people in the world to treat the dead bodies of their friends with neglect or disrespect, but during nearly half the year they were under the absolute necessity of putting their dead on scaffolds or abandoning them to wild beasts. Even after they became acquainted with the white men, they had no tools fit to dig graves with. It requires the best steel tools and men accustomed to use them, to dig graves in Minnesota in the depth of winter.

In the winter of 1834-5, a girl died at Lake Calhoun, and her friends, when leaving in March for the fur hunt, requested my brother and myself to bury her as soon as the ground should be thawed. We attempted to dig the grave in the beginning of April, but found the ground still frozen. As we had nothing better than a spade to dig with, we had to wait for the ground to thaw. Probably the Indians thought it impossible for them to dig graves in winter, and it certainly must have been so until they had iron tools. They would have needed graves themselves before they would have got through the frozen ground with their tools of wood or stone, either in Minnesota or British America.

Having once placed the bodies on the scaffolds, they were apt to leave them there too long. Sometimes they buried them as soon as they could, but most of the men, or frequently all, were absent from their villages, hunting furs or making sugar, until late in May, and then the burying was a disagreeable undertaking. Many who died in summer were buried when they died, while others were placed on scaffolds. Some, when they were sick, influenced by that natural dread of being buried in the earth which is felt by some white people, requested their friends to place their bodies on scaffolds. Others wished to be buried as soon as they were dead.

Being compelled by necessity to deposit corpses on scaffolds in the winter, they were familiar with the sight of them there, and it was perhaps natural that they should learn to place some of them there in summer; yet I think we may reasonably conclude that, if the ground had never been frozen where they lived, they would have buried their dead when they died, though now, if they were removed to a tropical country, they might in some instances keep the bodies of their friends above ground before burying them.

The dead were interred without any particular ceremony, in shallow graves two or three feet deep. The graves were protected by picket fences or by setting a row of posts on each side of the grave, leaning against each other at the top over the grave, the ends of the grave being protected by upright posts. These posts were set up as a protection against wild beasts.

The Dakotas selected elevated locations for burying places, and commonly set up poles by the graves of those recently buried, with pieces of white cloth tied to the tops like flags. These streamers were left to flutter in the wind till worn out. When a man of distinction died, if they could obtain a United States flag, they left it waving over his grave.

Besides the cloths that were wrapped around the dead, other things which had belonged to them were sometimes buried with them. Once at the burial of a boy, I saw his bow and arrows buried with him, and asked his mother, who was standing by, why it was done; she replied, "Whenever I see them, my grief will be renewed, and I want them buried out of sight." I understood her at once, and did not think it necessary to ask her any other questions. Though a squaw, she was a woman and a bereaved mother, and many white mothers have felt as she did. The cradles of infants were frequently deposited on the scaffold or in the grave when the babe died.

George Catlin says: "The Dakota mother, when she loses an infant, carries its cradle around with her a year or more, treating it the same as if the babe was in it." No such custom prevailed here, and indeed Mr. Catlin, during his short sojourn among the

Indians, discovered many things that have eluded the careful research of others. One can hardly help suspecting that

> "He was blest with optics keen
> For seeing what can ne'er be seen."

Food was deposited on the graves or scaffolds of those who had recently died, for a considerable time after their death. No regular supply of food was furnished, but occasionally a dish of choice viands was carried to the grave. After the food had stood a little while by the grave, it was commonly eaten, but not by those who placed it there. They did not imagine that the ghosts ate the food, but some who had a metaphysical turn of mind, when asked why it was placed there, said that food itself might have a spiritual part, which nourished the soul of the departed. This was an ingenious answer to those who complained of the absurdity of the custom, but is not to be received as the opinion of the common people, who probably had no opinion about it. I never felt disposed to be inquisitive about such things, for I never expected either white people or Indians to give logical reasons for all they did for their deceased friends.

The offerings made by them at the graves of their departed friends, like the flowers planted or strewn on the graves of our loved ones, are to be regarded as offerings of affection, and not as something to be explained or justified by a course of reasoning. Neither the food given by the Dakotas, nor the flowers which we plant, can benefit the dead. They can no more smell the fragrance of the blossoms than they can taste of the food. Such offerings show, and are only intended to show, that we would do something for the loved ones who have gone from us, if it were in our power. Let us not criticise too severely a custom of the Dakotas, which is only the counterpart of a custom so much cherished among ourselves. We may think that our own way of expressing a regard for the dead is better than theirs, but they are both alike manifestations of a sentiment that is common to all and dishonorable to none, both alike useless to the dead and honorable to the living.

A white woman of my acquaintance, who had but little property, purchased a very expensive coffin for her husband, and, when some one complained of her extravagance, she said: "It is all I can do for him." When we objected to making coffins large enough to contain all the cloths that the Dakotas wished to wrap around their dead, they looked grieved, and if they had expressed their feelings doubtless they would have said, "It is all we can do for them." Even now, while I am writing, their grieved, sad countenances come back to my remembrance, just as I saw them more than thirty years ago.

Some of the practices of the Dakotas reminded us of customs of the ancients, described or alluded to by Greek and Roman writers. The reader of Virgil knows that the custom of depositing food by graves, or of inviting ghosts to participate at feasts, was not peculiar to the Dakotas. They had also something like the funeral games of the ancients, where presents were distributed to the competitors. Sometimes when a man lost a son, he invited those who had been the boy's companions to play a game of ball in honor of their dead comrade, and at the close of the game distributed among them valuable presents.

When the Dakotas lost a near relative, they mourned with bitter and long-continued lamentations. They also blackened their faces, cut off their hair, and wounded themselves with knives or flints. There were different degrees of mourning, according as the deceased was nearly or more remotely related to the mourner, just as with us there are different degrees or grades of mourning apparel.

The most grievous mourning was that of a woman for her deceased husband. As soon as he was dead she cut off her hair to her neck, gave away her ornaments and valuable clothing, and mourned with loud lamentations. The women did not blacken their faces, but the men painted their faces black; and sometimes, but not often, the men made deep wounds in the flesh of their arms with knives. The women, with sharp pieces of flint, scarified their legs below the knees, until they were covered with blood which trickled down to the ground.

The mourning of a woman was about the same when she lost a child as when her husband died. On the death of her husband, the widow not only gave away her best clothing or exchanged it for meaner garments, but also gave away almost everything she had. If she did not give it away, some of her neighbors took it under the pretence that she was so absorbed with grief that she would no longer value it. She might be unwilling to part with some of the articles taken from her, but did not like to refuse anything that was asked for; otherwise it might be said that she cared more for her property than for her husband. They, however, sometimes complained to us that things were taken from them which they could not well spare.

Some of them felt reckless about their property, and for a time cared little who had it. To prevent its being lost, it was sometimes taken by friends of the widow, and was restored to her when her paroxysm of grief was over. A widow, mourning for her husband, presented for months the most desolate spectacle that can be imagined. Clothed in squalid garments, with her short disheveled hair hanging over her face, she joined in no diversions and spent much of the time wailing by her husband's grave. She wept till she was almost blind, and wailed till she was so hoarse that she could hardly speak. The manifestations of grief were much the same when women mourned for their children.

The mourning of the men resembled that of the women, but their demonstrations of grief were not so violent, and they wailed less in the day time, though they sat often and long by the graves of their wives and children.

All the kindred of the dead, to a remote degree of relationship, were among the mourners; and nearly all the inhabitants of a village might be and often were mourning at one time. The wailing commenced the instant a person died; and sudden, loud lamentations announced his death.

There was also a sudden outburst of wailing when the tidings were brought of the death of a relative in some distant place. The wailing consisted in singing or chanting a tune, in a voice sometimes mournful, sometimes wild, and in notes now very loud and again so low as to be scarcely audible, the mourners often calling on the deceased.

All mourners sang the same tune, but when many were wailing together they took little pains to sing in concert so as to produce harmony. Each lamented by himself, paying little attention to others, so that the mourning seemed less artificial and affected than if there had been a harmonious agreement of the voices of the mourners.

Few words were used in these lamentations.   A woman wailing for her child would repeat the words, Me choonk she! me choonk she! (My child, my child, My son, my son, or, My daughter, my daughter), a hundred times in succession, but usually said nothing more.   Men would occasionally utter, in a wild rapid manner, a sentence or two, which seemed to be extemporized; but commonly little was heard from the mourners, save the notes of the same invariable tune.   As there were usually a great many mourners for each of the dead, and as many of them mourned a long time, the mourners were always going about the streets.   By night these lamentations had an exceedingly sad and mournful sound, and there were few nights in which they were not heard.

The mourning of the Dakotas, though so different from our own, resembles that of some oriental nations, and reminds us of that of the ancient Hebrews.   The reason they gave for inflicting wounds on themselves was that the pain thus caused lessened their grief by diverting their minds from it.   This practice seems to have prevailed among the Israelites in Egypt, for it was forbidden by the law of Moses.   Little could be known of the real feelings of the mourners by these outward manifestations of grief, for they were no surer indications of sorrow than are the habiliments of mourning worn by us.

If a Dakota woman at the death of her husband had refused to cut off her hair and dress in rags, she would have appeared to her people in the same light as a white woman would to us, if, instead of putting on mourning garments when her husband died, she should immediately array herself in gay apparel.   I have heard the conduct of Dakota women criticised, when they failed to cut their hair quite so short as the fashion required or dressed a little better than became a widow, just as we hear complaints of white women who do not seem to feel the loss of their husbands quite so much or quite so long as they should.

The wailing which has been described was not confined to mourning for the dead.   It might be heard at any time from those who were sad and desponding.   The tune used by those who mourned for the dead was used also to give expression to any sad or disconsolate feelings.   In a large village or camp, there was scarcely a time when this melancholy tune might not be heard, especially in the night. The Dakotas were sometimes merry, but oftener sad. Though there was among them much singing and mirth, there was more wailing and lamentation.

When one died, a lock of his hair was preserved to be carried by a war party and left if possible where an enemy was killed. Their grief often had much of anger in it. Sorrow for the death of their friends was sometimes mingled with bitter, revengeful feelings and a desire to wreak vengeance on some one. As the Ojibways were always legitimate objects of vengeance, it was natural for them to wish to vent their spite on them.

The Dakota word which signifies to mourn is derived from the word anger, and it is to be feared that they were not the only ones who have a little of the bitterness of anger mixed with their grief. A half-breed of my acquaintance, who had received his education among white people and had no regard for Indian superstitions, was so provoked by the death of an only son that he sent a company of Indians against the Ojibways with a lock of the child's hair. This custom doubtless had its origin in angry, revengeful feelings, but it was universally adopted. The hair was wrapped in cloth and carefully preserved, the bundle hanging in some conspicuous place, generally with a consecrated spear, until there was an opportunity of sending it into the country of the enemy.

TRAFFIC AND PRESENTS.

The Dakotas exchanged articles of property to a considerable extent among themselves, but this traffic differed in some respects from trade as it is carried on by white people. All trade among them consisted in the exchange of goods, but nothing had a fixed value, and in bartering they did not always have regard to the relative value of the goods exchanged. If one wanted to get possession of something of value belonging to another, he might make the owner of the desired property a present, at the same time intimating that he should like to obtain the thing sought for; or he might wait a while, after conferring the present, before making his request. The article given might be of more or of less value than the one expected in return, but that did not always prevent an exchange.

The owner of the desired property might wish to keep it or it might be of much greater value than the present and it was sometimes refused, but Dakotas did not like to disoblige those who had given them presents.

Sometimes the offer was gladly accepted, for the thing given might be much more valuable than that which was asked in return. In their dealings with each other, there was not much sharp practice, and they had a very careless way of making bargains; but in their dealings with white men they were more particular and had no scruples about taking all they could get.

Hon. Norman W. Kittson once remarked to the writer that when an Indian brought him ducks, he wanted twice their value, and then was not satisfied unless he waited till they were cooked and ate them up, with as much more food besides. He had probably just been annoyed by a visit from some of his unreasonable customers, and this statement may have been exaggerated; but it had some foundation in fact, for they thought the resources of a white man inexhaustible.

In dealing with traders, they made the best bargain they could. That was the rule in this part of the country, but I was told by one of Mr. Renville's sons that in dealing with the buffalo hunters west of Lac qui Parle he did not set a price on his goods, but gave them to the chiefs, who distributed them among his people and collected their robes for the traders. No such methods, however, were used among the Dakotas on the Mississippi and Minnesota rivers, and probably not to any great extent farther west.

There were few or none of the Dakotas who made a practice of trading with their neighbors for the purpose of gain. The principal traffic of these Indians was with the buffalo hunters, from whom they received tents, buffalo robes, and horses, in exchange for goods purchased from the traders.

I have spoken of the presents given for the purpose of obtaining something in return for them. These are what our New England ancestors learned to call "Indian gifts." They, however, gave many valuable presents, asking nothing in return except a public acknowledgment. Whoever received a present of this kind, walked about the camp, singing a tune only used on such occasions. When he had gained the attention of the people, he proclaimed in a loud voice the name of the donor, saying, "Such a person has given me such a present and made me glad." This was repeated often for many days. The presents thus given were often things of value, such as guns and horses. They were sometimes given to the poor, who greatly needed them, and I have known horses presented to those who were lame. Some of their gifts were bestowed upon the rich, if any of them could be called rich. When young women, who were too bashful to sing alone in public, were recipients of these presents, they made their acknowledgments, with trembling voices, after dark.

Besides this ostentatious display of generosity or ability or vanity, bona fide presents were given by friends and relatives to each other much more than among us. There was much also given to the poor, such as widows and orphans, especially of food, for none were ever suffered to starve if there were provisions in the camp.

When a woman fed her own family, she also fed all who were present; and when game was brought in, a portion was sent to those who had none. Collections were taken for those who were very destitute. Travelers also were entertained and could pass without scrip or purse from one end of the country to the other. The generosity and hospitality of savages, which have been so highly extolled, were necessities of their condition, and without them they could not exist, for there were none among them who were not sometimes dependent upon others. The best hunter may become disabled and unable to support his family; and there is no coin current that the traveler can carry with him to defray the expenses of his journey.

It was customary for two persons to enter into intimate relations of friendship. The two persons thus bound to each other by the mutual promise of friendship were expected to have a particular regard for each other's welfare; and each was bound to stand by his friend and aid him in all times of necessity. This treaty of amity was ratified by an exchange of presents, and frequently by an exchange of garments and weapons, like that mentioned of David and Jonathan, even to "the sword and the girdle and the bow." Persons united in this covenant of friendship were very generous to each other.

The traffic of the Dakotas among themselves has been mentioned, but their trade was of course chiefly with the fur traders, from whom they received many of the necessaries of life. Though their ancestors contrived to do without these things, they had now become indispensable. They understood very well their dependence on fur traders, and there was no other subject to which their chiefs so often alluded in their speeches. On all occasions, the young men were warned not to do any mischief to the whites lest the trade should be interrupted. They had once long ago suffered severely in consequence of the withdrawal of the traders, caused by the murder of one of their number, and they never forgot the lesson. When their supply of ammunition was cut off, they were not only unable to use fire-arms in hunting, but they were at the mercy of their enemies. Shakopee could hardly make a speech to his people on any occasion without reminding them of their dependence on the whites.

There is a belief, generally prevalent, that the goods furnished to the Indians were of little value, consisting chiefly of paints, beads, earrings, and other trinkets; but that has not been the case in Minnesota for a long time, if ever. They received annually from the traders large quantities of valuable goods. Their blankets and other clothing were strong and durable, made expressly for them, and just such as they needed. The same is true of all the weapons and tools which were furnished to them. Their guns, kettles, axes, hoes, etc., were well adapted to their wants. Most of their peltries went to pay for such articles as have been mentioned, and but a small portion for ornaments.

With regard to the prices paid for these goods, the fur merchants doubtless made what profits they could, but there was no monopoly of the trade. On the contrary, there was spirited competition, and no such combination of the merchants to keep up or keep down prices as is so common among us at the present day. The trader was as anxious to buy a great many furs as to buy them cheap, and the Indians knew enough to carry their peltries where they could get the most for them.

As a class the men engaged in the fur trade were as honorable and fair in their dealings as the generality of men engaged in mercantile business; and, if there were rogues among them, there were also rogues among the Indians, who were quite a match for them.

Indians are not so easily cheated as some imagine. Whiskey-sellers could circumvent and rob their drunken customers, but there was no whiskey used in the legitimate trade, and sober Dakotas were generally quite competent to take care of themselves. They obtained most of their goods in advance, and a majority of them were tolerably honest and paid their debts if they could; but some were sharp enough, or roguish enough, to take goods from one trader and sell their furs to another.

In what is here said of the characters of the traders the writer has no reference to that class of persons who commenced their dealings with the Indians by selling them whiskey, and who took out licenses for trade only that they might share with the legitimate traders in the money appropriation for the payment of debts incurred by the Indians.

With regard to the money given by the government to the traders in the treaties of 1851, to cancel the unpaid debts of the Indians, the private opinion of the writer is that many of them got a little too much of it, but it is also his opinion that there are few who would not have taken it under the same circumstances.

TRADITIONS.

Considerable traditionary information might have been obtained from the Indians in 1834, but probably no one has taken the pains to collect or preserve it, and now it is too late. During the ensuing thirty years, the Dakotas of Minnesota have experienced strange vicissitudes of fortune, such as were calculated to turn their thoughts from the things that formerly engaged their attention. In the midst of the exciting scenes attending and following the Sioux Outbreak, and harassed with anxiety about the future, they have had no time to think of the past or give much heed to the traditions of their fathers. The young men have had their minds occupied with things new and strange, and the old men who had treasured up in their memories things of the past are all gone.

I always felt an interest in the fragments of their past history which had floated down to us on the tide of time, but failed to make a record of them, thinking it could be done at any time, for I anticipated no such changes as have taken place so rapidly. I will, however, mention here such of their traditions as I happen to remember.

It was believed by them that they came here from the north, and they may have formerly lived very far north, as they were acquainted with some of the habits of the Esquimaux, for whom they had a name, calling them "Eaters of raw food." They might have received their knowledge of the Esquimaux from other tribes, but their knowledge of Indian tribes did not extend so far in any other direction.

When first discovered by the French, many of them were living northwest of Lake Superior, and some of the Assiniboines, who are also Dakotas, were living still farther north. Indeed, they could have come into this country from Asia only by going as far north as the Arctic circle. The Ojibways boast of having driven them down from the north; and they, of having expelled the Iowas from the country bordering on the Mississippi and Minnesota rivers.

The Ojibways obtained fire-arms sooner than the Dakotas, and therefore were able to drive them out of the wooded country about the sources of the Mississippi and Rum rivers. If they had come into possession of fire-arms as early as their enemies did, it is not probable that they would have lost any of their lands.

In the year 1695 a Dakota chief, accompanying Le Sueur, was the first of his nation to visit Canada. He went to beg for weapons, and said to Frontenac, "All the nations have a father who protects them. All have iron weapons; pity me, for I have none."

The Dakotas did not like to say much about having been expelled from a portion of their land by "the thick lips," as they in derision called the Ojibways; but they often spoke of having driven the Iowas from southern Minnesota. They did not speak of this as some ancient tradition, but as a well known event of comparatively recent occurrence, though it must have taken place more than two hundred years ago. This proves that important events were not soon forgotten by them. How long it is since the Iowas were here cannot now be known. Le Sueur said they dwelt near what is now the boundary between Minnesota and Iowa, in the latter part of the seventeenth century.

The small mounds, which may be seen on the left bank of the Minnesota at Eden Prairie and Bloomington, and perhaps at other places, are, the Dakotas say, the ruins of dwelling houses built by the Iowas. These mounds are in rows or groups, on the bluff of the northwest side of the river. They are circular and of various sizes. I never measured them, and it is long since I have seen them; but I think they are three or four feet high and fifteen to twenty feet in diameter at the base. Their situation on the north side of the river, if there are none on the south side, indicates that the Iowas were more apprehensive of an attack from the south than from the north. They may have been formerly on friendly terms with the Dakotas, as they sometimes were after their removal from this section.

At Bloomington I saw one of these mounds opened, and discovered no reason why the statement of the Dakotas concerning their origin and use might not be correct. It had evidently been built of turf, supported by a wooden frame and destroyed by burning the frame. It was composed of dark soil, which could be obtained there only from the surface of the ground, for the black surface soil rested on a substratum of yellowish sand, the surface soil being so thin that most of it would be taken up with the turf. The charred remains of several sticks of timber, six inches or more in diameter, were lying parallel to each other across the bottom of the mound. If there had been smaller sticks in the frame, they had been consumed. The turf covering doubtless prevented the larger timbers from being burnt to ashes. At the bottom of the mound, on a level with the general surface of the earth, were the bones of a human body, which, on being removed, crumbled to dust except some of the teeth. These bones were deeper in the earth than the Dakotas were accustomed to bury.

The general rendezvous of the Medawakantonwan was, at no remote period, on the north bank of the Minnesota river, a little below the mouth of the Nine Mile creek. There they were secure from the attacks of their enemies, being protected on one side by the river and on the other by a lake several miles in length. It was probably only a place where they occasionally met, for, as they did not plant, they could not continue long in one place. This division of the Dakotas derived its name from Mde wakan (Spirit Lake, now called Mille Lacs); and the general name of the Dakotas of Minnesota was derived from a lake which they called Isanta-mde (Knife lake), in Kanabec county, about fifteen miles southeast of Mille Lacs. Neither of these places has been in their possession for generations, but they are often referred to in their traditionary legends.

Warlike events made the deepest and most lasting impression on the minds of the Dakotas, and were as in other nations held in longest remembrance. They were in the habit of recounting the various vicissitudes of war, whether fortunate or adverse; and no important battle, whether successful or unsuccessful, was soon forgotten. They related with minute exactness all the particulars of their victories and defeats, and if they had been able to preserve the dates of events, they could have furnished materials for an interesting history of the wars in which their nation had been engaged. They had, however, no way of preserving dates farther back than three or four generations. Of all more ancient events they could only say, "That happened long ago."

The time which had elapsed since the occurrence of more recent events they measured not by years but by generations. So they would say of an event that it happened in the time of their father, grandfather, or great grandfather, but did not go back more than three or four generations. They used to speak of an assault made by the Ojibways on one of their camps, in which many of the Dakotas were killed or wounded, though they finally repulsed their assailants; and, when asked how long ago the affair happened, would refer to an old man, then living, and say that he was born during the fight, and that a kettle was put over him as a shield. This was more exact than most of their dates; when we saw the old man we could only guess at his age, but we knew how old he was when the fight took place.

They did not pretend to keep a record of time for any great number of years, and few of the older ones knew exactly their own ages; but long after the dates were lost, the facts themselves might be carefully preserved in memory. I have heard all the vicissitudes of a battle, with the names and exploits of the chief actors, minutely and graphically described, when the narrator could neither tell nor guess within hundreds of years of the time when the battle was fought. Sometimes the kinds of weapons used by the combatants determined the question whether the fight took place before or after they were furnished with fire-arms.

These stories were doubtless true accounts of real events, for they were careful to relate them to their children just as they received them from their fathers. If any narrator happened to differ a little from the common version, his account was scrutinized as closely as an unusual reading of Virgil or Homer is by the classical critics. I have heard many of these legends, but have no such distinct remembrance of them as would justify me in attempting to relate them to others.

It has been already mentioned that the Dakotas had a great store of anecdotes, short accounts of anything which they thought worth remembering. Some of these are serious, some humorous; and they were used by them, as similar tales are used by us, for amusement, illustration, or instruction.

One of these tales gives an example of remarkable presence of mind in a female. As a woman was one night standing by a kettle of oil, with a torch shining upon it, she saw, as in a mirror, one of their enemies' scouts peeping through an aperture in the tent. Without changing her position or manifesting any alarm she told her husband in a low voice what she saw, who seized his weapon and killed the dangerous visitor before he suspected that he was discovered. The reader can receive this as a fact or a fable. It either shows wonderful self-possession in a woman, or a genius for invention on the part of the narrator not much less remarkable. Some of these anecdotes were witty, exciting mirth; and others were grave, designed to convey instruction.

They had proverbs, current sayings, some of which were quite apt; for instances, "The elbow is the bravest part of the body, the eye the most cowardly," and "No man who is absent from a battle would not have been brave if he had been there, and no man who is not present at a council would not have been wise had he been there."

They were in the habit of often speaking of the things manufactured by their ancestors before the arrival of traders with implements of iron. Indeed, in 1834 it was only about one hundred and eighty years since any of them first saw a white man; and it must have been much later before their stone weapons, earthen kettles, etc., were superseded and discarded, so that it would have been strange if the remembrance of them had been lost in oblivion. They could give a minute description of the rude tools their fathers had used before they obtained iron. They knew how fire was kindled without the fire-steel. They also knew how fishhooks were made by joining together pieces of bones. They told of various ways in which spear and arrow heads were made of horn, bone, etc., and also described the pottery manufactured by their fathers, their earthen kettles as they called them, which they said were very useful and convenient, but too heavy and fragile to compete with iron ones. One of these earthen kettles was found in a cave at Shakopee.

I was surprised to learn from the Dakotas that they did not believe their ancestors had ever used stone arrowheads. They knew so well what utensils and weapons were formerly used by their people that this seeming ignorance about the arrowheads puzzled me, for I supposed of course they had all used flints for arrow points. Some of the Dakotas we know used them, but these Dakotas used bone and horn for arrow points, and perhaps did not use flint for that purpose at all. Stone points for arrows and spears could not have been much used in this section by any people, for they are very rare. I have found more of them on one farm in New England than all that I have seen in Minnesota.

According to their own testimony, a usage formerly prevailed among the Dakotas, which, though not much to their credit, was characteristic of this people, namely, their singular way of disposing of those who were superannuated and unable to keep along with hunting parties. They were unable or unwilling to carry them, and had some scruples about killing them without ceremony or leaving them to perish by slow degrees; so they compromised the matter, and did what they called "making enemies" of them. The old men were armed with guns or bows and arrows and were allowed to defend themselves as well as they could, while the young men killed them with clubs. They thus gave them an opportunity to die with honor on the field of battle, and satisfied their scruples of conscience about killing them. This custom has long been obsolete, but it was not discontinued in consequence of a change in the disposition of the people. Probably there were not many of the old men who would not have chosen rather to be killed as enemies than to be left to perish by starvation. The old women, I suppose, were not killed; but some of them were left to die, and I have in later times known one or two to perish from intentional neglect. The aged were, however, generally treated kindly.

Among the traditionary tales which I have preserved in manuscript, there are two in which mention is made of old women who were left behind to die. In one case, a young man, when he discovered that an old woman was left alone at a deserted camp, took her on his back, and, walking with his burden, joined the rest of the company. The young people, male and female, all made sport of him, and his father and uncle entreated him not to disgrace himself and them by carrying an old woman on his back. To this he replied: "I see no disgrace in having compassion on the wretched; I think the disgrace belongs to those who left this old woman to die; and though she is a wrinkled, shriveled old thing, I will not desert her, even if we be attacked by an enemy on the way." He soon had an opportunity to make his promise good, for they were attacked the same day, during their march; but while the rest of the party took to flight, he laid the old woman down on the ground, and, standing over her, killed some of the assailants and put the rest to flight. The people now proposed to make him chief, as a reward for his valor; but he declined the offer, and told them that whatever honors they designed for him, they might bestow upon the old woman. She was accordingly treated with the greatest respect as long as she lived.

The story about the other old woman is that she was left in the fall of the year to die, and when those who deserted her returned in the spring, as they passed near the place where she was left, some of the young men said, "Let us go and look at the old woman's bones." Instead of finding her bones gnawed by the wolves, they found her alive and abundantly supplied with provisions; for, during the whole winter, a compassionate hunter had made long journeys to supply her wants. I am sorry that, in order to tell the whole story, I am compelled to add that the scoundrels killed her and took her provisions.

Such stories as these prove that there were some Dakotas who knew how to show compassion, or else that there were some who knew how to describe it. I have made mention in this work of many things that are in themselves trivial and unworthy of notice except as they help to illustrate the character of the Indians.

Most persons who know anything about the Dakotas, have heard of the girl who leaped from the precipice now called Maiden Rock, to avoid marrying a man whom she disliked. The story is credible, for others have committed suicide for the same reason.

All have heard of the Dakota woman who went in a canoe with her child over the Falls of St. Anthony. A poem penned by the present writer in the year 1850 tells the story of An-pe-tu-sa-pa-win, substantially as it was related by the Dakotas. The efforts of the mother to encourage her child, as they drew near the cataract, which I consider an incident of touching interest, is part of the original story, as is that which relates to the paint and other adornings of herself and child, and also the death song.*

CONCLUDING REMARKS.

The author of this work does not imagine that he has succeeded in giving a perfect description of the Dakotas, for no one who was not himself bred an Indian from childhood knows just what they are. He has been particular to notice such things as he thought would most clearly illustrate the Indian character, and many of their practices have been described which exhibit them in a very unfavorable light.

The reader should not conclude that they were fools because they had foolish notions or foolish practices, for the wisest of pagans had notions and customs as foolish. Does not Xenophon tell us that he rejoiced at the good omen when one of his soldiers happened to sneeze at the right time? And did not the old Romans watch the flight of birds, and carefully inspect the entrails of calves and pigs, to discover whether an army should march or halt, whether it should fight or avoid a battle? Yet Xenophon was a great general and a great writer, and the founders of the Roman Empire were not fools. Rousseau says, "The most contemptible divinities were served by the greatest men."

It would be easy, by making prominent one class of facts and suppressing another, to exhibit the Dakotas as worthy of admiration, or as little better than incarnate fiends. Their traits of

---

*This poem, "An-pe-tu-sa-win, a Legend of the Dakotas," was published in an article entitled "Saint Paul and its Environs," by Rev. Edward D. Neill, in Graham's Magazine (Vol XLVI, pp. 3-17, January, 1855), and in "Two Volunteer Missionaries among the Dakotas," by S. W. Pond, Jr. (1893, pp. 273-278).

character, both good and bad, were strongly marked; and their appearance at different times was so different that they could hardly be recognized as the same persons. The appearance of a conjurer howling over a sick person was so hateful and revolting that one shrank from him, as from the presence of a demon; and yet, an hour after, you might find the same man an intelligent, good-natured companion.

One day, a woman might be seen trotting around the circle in the wakan dance, and throwing herself on the ground like one demented; and the next day she was at home assiduously engaged in the discharge of her duties as a wife and mother, and kindly attentive to the wants of herself and family.

There was a dark side to this people, exceedingly dark. They were not so amiable as to render it desirable for a white person of a timid and yielding disposition to reside among them, and those who were easily circumvented and imposed upon should never take up their abode with wild Dakotas. Being quick to discover all the weak points of those with whom they had to deal, they knew how to approach, whether with flatteries, menaces, or falsehoods. They flattered the vain and proud, frightened the timid, and deceived the simple. Many of them were neither too proud to beg nor too good to steal, and he was a shrewd man whom they did not sometimes deceive.

Unable to appreciate the benevolent motives of those who treated them kindly, they retained no grateful remembrance of benefits received and often returned evil for good. Hard and stoical in their tempers, they felt little sympathy for the sufferings of others, were more ready to laugh at mistakes than to pity misfortunes, and often, in an object deserving pity, could see only a source of mirth. What are tragedies with us, were comedies with them. They did not seem to know that beasts and birds had any feelings, and they could make sport of the dying agonies of their fellow men.

Their religious beliefs, as taught them by their prophets, were a strange medley of silly whims and abominable falsehoods; and their superstitious practices were a compound of ludicrous follies and disgusting absurdities. And still, in the midst of this degradation, they were, in their own conceit, too wise to be taught, and too nearly perfect to need improvement. Their religion was deemed superior to all others, and their prophets the wisest of mortals. This is the dark side of the picture, and it might be made still darker without exaggeration; but there was a brighter side which should not be left out.

The longer we lived among them, the more we were made to feel that Indians and squaws are men and women, possessing many redeeming traits of character, and by no means sunk to the lowest depths of degradation. When these rude barbarians are tried by a faultless standard, or are compared with those who have attained to a high degree of civilization, they appear to disadvantage; but they lose nothing by comparison with any other savage people, ancient or modern, not excepting our own pagan ancestors. Compared with the naked, lascivious natives of Africa and the islands of the Pacific, their character was noble and their manners decent and becoming.

It is true that they were savage hunters, but what else could they be? There was not an animal in all America that has been found worth taming, except the dog and the little llama of Peru, not one that could be made to draw a plow or cart, or to carry a burden on its back. Some of the animals of America have strength enough, but their spirits are indomitable. Men do not plow with the elk, the bison or buffalo, or the grizzly bear. A civilized people without domestic animals would be something new in the history of our race. We can hardly blame Indians for not doing what has never been done by any other people.

Though the Indians did not themselves extensively cultivate the soil, they prepared the way for those who do. If America had been without human inhabitants, every acre of fertile soil in the valley of the Mississippi would have been covered with dense forests. There would be no present demand for reaping machines in Minnesota. In denuding the land of timber, by setting fires, to give pasturage for the buffalo, elk, and deer, the Indians did their work too thoroughly in some places; but they saved the civilized settlers of the country the work of generations. The world has no reason to regret that they were ignorant of that kind of civilization which increases the numbers without improving the morals of a people.

It is not strange that the Indians do not at once adopt the habits and conform to the customs of civilized people. The process of civilization is always a slow one. It has taken the white man thirty generations to attain to his present position, and we can hardly expect that the Indian will overtake him at once. It is the misfortune of the Dakota, not his fault, that he is so far behind in the race of civilization.

While for many generations we have been walking in the light, he has been wandering in darkness, and he is dazzled and bewildered by the new light which shines so suddenly around him. He finds himself unfitted for his new position, unable to cope with his white neighbor, and is discouraged. There is danger that he will give up to this feeling of despondency, as many others of his race have done, and not try to imitate those whom he cannot hope to equal; for an Indian never likes to do anything which others can do better than he, and would rather have the reputation of being indolent than that of being awkward. The Dakota has capabilities and he knows it, but they are not of the kind to fit him for his new situation. He is as much out of place as the farmer would be, if compelled to become a hunter.

He knows that we have greatly the advantage of him, and, with all his apparent apathy, he feels it keenly. Let us be patient with him. He may be an object of pity, but not of scorn. He has in him all the elements of true manhood; let us not regard him as though he did not belong to the same race with ourselves.

There is a difference between him and us, for he is descended from a long line of hunters, and inherits the instincts and peculiarities of a hunter. While the Dakota follows the occupation of his ancestors, he has use for all those peculiar instincts and habits which he has derived from them. That hardihood of body and stoical fortitude of mind, which enable him to encounter hardships with resolution and endure suffering without repining, that watchfulness never remitted, that self-possession which never deserts him, that habit of observation which nothing can escape, and that sagacity or instinct that enables him to find his way, without chart or compass, through an unknown region,—all these things, and many more like them, are his inheritance, and they are of inestimable value to him so long as he remains a hunter, but when he turns his attention to some other employment their value is all gone.

As a man, he is by nature equal to the white man; as a hunter, he is superior; as a farmer, he is far inferior and feels his inferiority. It would be better for him, perhaps, if he were less conscious of it or less ashamed of it. It is a defect that cannot be immediately remedied, but the Dakota is probably as promising a candidate for civilization as our European ancestors were two thousand years ago. We may hope that he will improve faster than they did, for the world will not wait for him as long and as patiently as it did for them.

Some seem to imagine that the Dakotas have obstinately resisted all attempts to civilize them, but what efforts have been made in this direction and how long have they been continued? For a long time the only white men with whom the Dakotas had anything to do were fur traders, and they did not come here to civilize Indians. They did not bring to the natives plows and hoes, nor advise them to raise corn and wheat. They brought guns and traps, and asked for the skins of wild beasts. All the advice and encouragement which the Dakotas received from white men for a long series of years tended to confirm them in their habits as hunters. No one need be told that the fur trade and agriculture are antagonistic, and we could hardly expect that men who had all their capital invested in the fur trade would advise the Indians to stop hunting. Those who were engaged in the fur trade exercised a controlling influence over the Dakotas, and, while that influence continued, they did not remain uncivilized because they refused to listen to the advice of white men.

To relate what has since been done by the government for their civilization, does not come within the scope of this work. What was done for them while they were in Minnesota was badly planned and badly executed, and none could wonder that it was a failure and worse than a failure. With one hand the government presented to them plows, and with the other bestowed on them guns and ammunition. Which were they expected to use, the plows or the guns?

The plows were put in charge of white men, but the guns were put into their own hands. They were excluded from a great portion of their former hunting grounds, but were annually furnished with a superabundance of implements for hunting. They were never before so bountifully supplied with fire-arms, as at the very time when they were advised neither to hunt nor to make war. What were they expected to do with their guns?

They were advised to turn their attention to agriculture, but, as though to prevent their being stimulated by want to cultivate the earth, they were fed like paupers in a poor-house. If the Dakotas had been what they are not, the most docile people in the world, it would have been difficult for them to know just what our government wanted of them.

Let us not decide that the Dakota is incapable of being civilized till he has been fairly tried. During a manful struggle, continued through many generations, he has proved himself a match for all other enemies, and let us hope that civilization will not destroy him. There are many of these Dakotas left yet, some of them in all their native wildness; and, if they can be tamed, the race is one well worth preserving.

INDEX.